WESTHILL MEDIA
PUBLISHING

Who Murdered Diana?

Copyright 2021 by Stephen B. Ubaney

Writers Guild of America, West Inc.
7000 West Third Street
Los Angeles, CA 90048-4329
Voice: (323) 782-4500
  Fax: (323) 782-4803

Additional copies may be ordered at:

www.whomurderedbooks.com
https://www.facebook.com/Who-Murdered-Diana-1012378708786441
ISBN: 978-1-7333048-2-5 (Softcover)
ISBN: 978-1-7333048-3-2 (eBook)
The book is also available on Audiobook

Author's note

The *Who Murdered?* book series is the only one of its kind. It solves celebrity deaths, that are decades old, with new information revealing the painful truth that the people featured in its volumes were murdered.

These investigations take thousands of hours to complete producing suspects that are analyzed using the three elements of a crime; Motive, Means and Opportunity.

Decoding the lies of the past that were sold to the public when the flow of information was easier to control, is no easy task, but someone has to tell everyone the truth.

There is no Easter Bunny, there is no Tooth Fairy, there is no Santa Clause, and the people who are featured in this book series did not die as we were told.

This is the fourth volume in the *Who Murdered?* books series. The first three volumes: Who Murdered Elvis?, Who Murdered FDR?, and Who Murdered Elvis? 5th Anniversary Edition were great books; but this volume is quite different.

Diana's murder was more recent than those featured in the first three volumes and because of it, there was a treasure trove of facts, newspaper articles, books, and magazines that needed to be researched, chronicled, and investigated.

My most difficult task was to stay objective and "unlearn" the lies that have been parroted by the world's media since 1997. Once I surrendered to the facts of the case, I was shocked at how badly they wanted her dead and the extent that they went to kill her.

Although I fancy myself as more of a historical researcher and less of believer in vast conspiracies, I would be lying if I said that didn't encounter them, and this one bothered me weeks after the manuscript was completed. Enjoy the wild ride that this book will take you on, and in the end, all will be revealed.

Those who are thanked

Jerry McGarrity

Katarina Postl

Nova Wise

Daniel Eno

William Weller, Esq

Those who are acknowledged

Jim Ostrowski, Esq

Debora Becerra, Esq

Mark Lane, Esq

Gary White Esq

Eddie Van Halen

Those who inspired

Gerard Crinnin, PhD

Mark Lane, Esq

Richard Hugo

Robert Nasca Esq

The following manuscript was created at the expense of 3981 hours of research, investigation, and production labor.

1
The Chronicle

"I'd like to be queen of people's hearts, in people's hearts, but I don't see myself being Queen of this country. I don't think many people will want me to be Queen"

- Princess Diana: Panorama TV November 20th, 1995 -

As surely as the warm summer breeze turns into the autumn chill, so must volume IV in this book series must be written. The river of newfound truth, which I am so dedicated to, is flowing through me once again, as it has so many times in the past. I am often asked why I endeavor to write such books and investigate the death of these famous people decades after their demise.

There are so many answers to that question that I struggle to adequately reply. Among the flood of answers is my belief that I research and write these books to honor the people featured in them. There is so little justice and dignity left in this world that I almost feel a duty to reveal the truth about their murder, so they can finally rest in peace.

To solve Diana's murder, we must first understand her life and how she blossomed from obscurity to international stardom. This chapter is entitled The Chronicle because that's exactly what it does. It chronicles the factual and historical events about Diana Spencer from her childhood to her stardom.

Diana first appeared to the world on the arm of the heir apparent to the British throne, Prince Charles. Born in Buckingham palace on November 14th 1948, Charles is the eldest child of Queen Elizabeth II and will go down in history as the oldest and longest-serving heir apparent in British history.

He is the first grandchild of King George VI and Queen Elizabeth and was groomed to be king since he was a child. After earning a Bachelor of Arts degree from Trinity College in Cambridge, he was thrust into service in both the Royal Air Force and Royal Navy. For most of his life he had been poked and prodded by the crown to fulfill what would eventually be his birth rite.

As the third decade of his life came into being, he felt enormous pressure from the Queen to find a wife and become a father. The pressure came, not because of any deficiency in his choices, but the need to wed and sire children to expand the longevity of the royal family.

Like so many before him, he understood the double-edged sword that being born into royalty had cast upon him and he was less than enamored that his life had to fit within the confines of their boundaries.

Diana's childhood was a little different. A misconception about Diana is that she was born into an average family and was an English "commoner." In reality, she was anything but, as her family lineage was more pure than that of her future husband's. Diana's royal ancestry can be traced to the kings of England, as well as the kings of France.

In 1327 King Edward III claimed the English throne and ten years later he also became the king of France linking Diana to the royalty of both countries. This was also the case with the Windsor family and several generations later, Diana Spencer would marry her cousin, Prince Charles. This marriage was not a coincidence.

Diana Spencer was born into a privileged family on July 1, 1961 in Norfolk, England. Her father was the 8th Earl John Spencer and he was the product of generations of carefully guided British nobility, royal ancestry and planned breeding.

She grew up in Park House which is situated on the Sandringham estate approximately 90 miles north of London. The sprawling estate covers 20,000 acres of land and was to be the perfect place for Diana, and her five siblings to enjoy their slice of paradise. Unfortunately, her early years would be lived in emotional torment.

The year prior to her birth the family suffered the loss of an infant son and she was made to bear the brunt of this emotional scarring well into the next decade. Continuing the Spencer bloodline with male heirs is very important to a family of such nobility and having two male heirs to carry on their name was a necessity; a necessity that a female infant couldn't fulfil.

Years later, after her marriage to Prince Charles, Diana would come to realize the mounting pressure that royalty applies to a family to sire two boys so that the royal bloodline can continue. It was the second time that she would be made to feel this emotional pain.

Diana's birth was met with tears, but not of joy, of royal disappointment. This feeling of being unwanted would be made to haunt this beautiful little girl well past her formative years, and although her royal childhood was privileged, it was also emotionally bleak by the designed guilt of being born female.

Her childhood was littered with sadness as she tried to console her mother's tears, her father's bitter silence and tend to a brother who cried myself to sleep at night. Her feelings of guilt would soon be coupled with feelings of abandonment.

At the age of six, already painfully aware of her parent's violent fighting, she would become the product of a broken home as her parents filed for divorce. When the marital split finally happened, in 1969, her mother immediately remarried a man named Peter Shand Kydd, an heir to a wallpaper fortune, forcing Diana, her two sisters and her younger brother to live with her father.

Feeling emotionally victimized by her family once again, she slowly took on the role of caretaker to most of the siblings as she tried to make sense of their broken home. Diana's father was a loving man who had the financial means and support staff to properly care for his children, but there was no way for him to repair the emotional torment that his divorce had played upon their minds. The years spent under her father's rule were stable and filled with as much joy as he was able to provide until her forced ousting from her family at the age of nine.

At nine years old her primary home-schooling under the supervision of her governess, Gertrude Allen ended, and she was enrolled in Silfield Private School in Gayton, Norfolk. This all-girls boarding school would become her new home until the age of twelve where the homesick little girl would prove to be less than a satisfactory student.

After graduation she was shuffled off to her next schooling adventure joining her sisters at the exclusive West Heath Girls' School. There she was recognized for her community spirit, and her musical, dancing and swimming talent; but she displayed less than stellar grades and was still regarded as a remedial student by her educators.

In fact, her disinterest in schoolwork and lackluster scholastic performance often resulted in excessive tutoring and reprimand. It was becoming evident that all Diana wanted to do was to go home. It was during this restless time that Diana first met Prince Charles.

It was November of 1977 and she was on a much-needed break from school when she was introduced to the man touted as the world's most eligible bachelor by the royal press.

Charles had been dating her sister, Sarah, and she was introduced to the Prince at Althorp estates while he was target shooting with his friends. Diana, who was painfully shy, was completely unaware that the Prince had developed an interest in her and melted into the crowd.

She remembered him as a very solemn and sad looking man who was a romantic rebound for Sarah as she was nursing a broken heart over the loss of her romance to the Duke of Westminster. As Sarah's relationship with the Prince deepened, she was invited to his 30th birthday party at Buckingham Palace and much to her dismay, her little sister, Diana, was also invited.

Although the details of the relationship between the Prince and Sarah were sketchy at best, one thing is publicly known. Sarah made a comment about their relationship to a reporter for *The Mirror* named James Whittaker claiming that she had no interest in marrying Charles *"if he were the dustman or the King of England."* Such comments not only dented the ego of the Prince but the those behind the royal crest as well, and Charles ended the relationship in a huff.

Diana, now sixteen years old, returned to school and her lackluster academic performance continued as she failed all of the classes necessary for her certification for secondary school; not once, but twice. Still battling the emotional scars of childhood with the newfound responsibilities of adolescence, she was forced to drop out and was immediately enrolled in Institut Alpin Videmanette, a very posh finishing school.

There, nestled in the mountains of Switzerland, her miseries multiplied. Andrew Morton's book Diana: Her True Story – In Her Own Words, writes. *"I know that when I went to finishing school [the Institut Alpin Videmanette in Switzerland] I wrote something like 120 letters in the first month. I was so unhappy there - I just wrote and wrote and wrote. I felt out of place there. I learned how to ski but I wasn't very good with everybody else. It was just too claustrophobic for me, albeit it was in the mountains. I did one term there. When I found out how much it cost to send me there I told my parents it was a waste of their money. So they whipped me back."*

Diana was a social butterfly and was totally out of place in school. Much to her parents' chagrin, she got her way, and never returned to complete her schooling, leaving her with no qualifications or marketable skills to enter the workforce.

By Easter of 1978 Diana had returned to London where she shared her mother's apartment with two of her friends. To pay the bills she worked many jobs. She worked as a maid for her sisters, she acted as a hostess at parties, worked as a nanny, taught dance classes, and eventually landed a steady job as teacher's assistant at a preschool.

As a reward for her hard work, and for learning how to stand "on her own two feet", her mother bought her a flat of her own as a present for her 18th birthday. That is where she lived, with three of her friends as roommates, until fate intervened.

Although the Prince had known Diana for several years, they hadn't been in each other's company for some time. That changed in August of 1980 when he extended an invitation for her family to be his weekend guest at a polo tournament.

As she watched him play the Prince was struck by how quickly she had become a young woman and she was reintroduced to Charles by none other than Diana's sister, Sarah. Diana, who now possessed all of the attributes prized by a superficial male was ripe for the picking. The Prince, now thirty-two, was facing enormous pressure to marry and extend the royal bloodline, and the inevitable courtship began.

Diana had all of the hallmarks of a future queen. She was from an aristocratic family and she was a soft-spoken virgin without a reputation that would put the image of the royal family in jeopardy. With the blessing of Queen Elizabeth their relationship quickly progressed.

The Prince invited Diana to sail aboard the royal yacht Britannia for a weekend where the couple started to bond. This jaunt was quickly followed by an invitation to Balmoral Castle, the Windsor family's Scottish home, where Diana's charm far surpassed the expectations of the royal family. Six months later, on February 24th 1981, news of the royal engagement was made public and the whole of Europe celebrated the occasion.

Diana Recalls her proposal in an interview with Andrew Morton. *"Anyway, so he said: 'Will you marry me?' and I laughed. I remember thinking 'This is a joke', and I said: 'Yeah, OK', and laughed. He was deadly serious. He said: 'You do realize that one day you will be Queen.' And a voice said to me inside: 'You won't be Queen but you'll have a tough role.' So I thought: 'OK', so I said: 'Yes.' I said: 'I love you so much. I love you so much.' He said: 'Whatever love means. He said it then. So I thought that was great! I thought he means that! And so he ran upstairs and rang his mother."*

Per Royal tradition, the bride is allowed to select her engagement ring. Diana wasted no time in selecting a huge ring consisting of 14 solitaire diamonds surrounding a 12-carat oval sapphire in an 18-carat white gold setting. The ring was very similar to her mother's engagement ring, and the naive little girl, who'd buried all of her emotional scars from childhood, was on cloud nine.

Following the engagement Diana's life changed dramatically. The press, who had hounded her relentlessly throughout the entire courtship with Charles, had stepped up their game to match the fevered pitch of the entire population of the UK and all of its publications. Suddenly, everywhere Diana went she was having cameras stuck in her face and questions hurled at her. Reporters were desperately trying to learn anything that they could about this mystery girl who was suddenly next in line to be queen.

The Royal Family, who was equally ecstatic that Charles had fulfilled their long-desired wishes of marriage, extended a lifeline to Diana inviting her to live at Buckingham Palace until the wedding. Quickly accepting their offer to escape the constant pressures of the paparazzi, Diana left her job and tried to prepare herself for her new life as a "royal in waiting."

As they world went about their lives, buzzing with anticipation for the upcoming fairytale wedding, Diana cried her eyes out. In what seemed like a blink of an eye she was separated from her family, her friends, her flat and her newfound independence. She was living the fairytale that every little girl dreams of, but she was perfectly miserable doing it. If the imagery wasn't so sad, it would have been comical. A beautiful young princess sequestered away from the public behind huge rock walls in a drafty castle feeling as though life had abandoned her.

When she tried to speak to Charles about the immense and mounting pressure of transforming her life into royalty, he was unable to comfort her. Being royal was the only life that he knew and couldn't relate to her emotional struggle. To try and take her mind off of her peril, he frequently changed the subject telling her about what a tough time Camilla Parker Bowles was having accepting the wedding. Diana asked the same question that you're asking right now. Who the hell is Camilla Parker Bowles? That was the name of the woman that would come to haunt her every move and social event until her untimely death.

She had no idea that Camilla's romantic relationship with the Prince was far stronger than their relationship as it had extended far beyond friendship for many years. This added attraction compounded Diana's feelings of inadequacy and would mentally nag her throughout the length of her marriage.

Camilla was born on July 17th 1947 as Camilla Rosemary Shand and would marry Andrew Parker Bowles. Andrew was a Guards officer and lieutenant in the Blues and Royals cavalry regiment of the British Army and part of the Household Cavalry.

Camilla and Prince Charles met and became fast friends and lovers in 1971. Both were well known within their social circle and they regularly met when Charles played polo matches. As the relationship deepened, Charles met Camilla's family members, but the relationship was suddenly put on hold as Charles was pressed into service with the Royal Navy and was quickly shipped overseas.

It was later known that Queen Elizabeth disapproved of their relationship and she arranged for his quick military departure. Upon Charles' return from the Navy their promiscuous relationship resumed and continued throughout Camilla's marriage. Palace courtiers reported the situation to the Queen who was pressuring Charles to marry, but saw Camilla as unsuitable as a wife for the future king. For their marriage to happen she would need to be divorced and she was obviously not a virgin.

Both of these issues were major obstacles and were not allowed by the creed of the Royal Family who conducted themselves by certain rules, very old rules. Instead, the Queen was pressuring Charles to marry one of his cousins in the Spencer family who had been grooming their girls from childhood to be the wives of royalty. The queen knew that they were prime marrying stock and that they were all virgins.

The bitter truth was that Diana had been selected by the Queen - not Charles. This revelation would eventually be discovered by Diana in the most painful of ways beginning with the ramp up to the most glorious of weddings in more than one hundred years. Diana had no way of knowing the mess that she was marrying into.

All she knew was that she was marrying into royalty and her first public appearance with Prince Charles was at a recital at London's Goldsmith's Hall. It was March of 1981 and Diana appeared wearing a strapless black taffeta dress with a plunging neckline. This was a stunning departure from her regular attire and was the beginning of the media's obsession with her.

The "blushing bride" to be could barely contain her glee as she had the honor or meeting Grace Kelly, the Princess of Monaco, who privately told her to be careful of the world that she was marrying into. It was Diana's night to shine and everyone from Prince Charles, to the Royal Family, to the onlookers of the globe couldn't have been happier.

It was a time before social media, 24-hour news channels or the option of "cutting the cord" like so many have done with cable TV. All eyes were on this fairytale couple as the world seemed to live vicariously through their every move as the wedding of a lifetime approached. In the weeks preceding the wedding Charles continued to see Camilla getting caught at every turn while the palace was desperately trying to keep the affair hidden.

Meanwhile, Charles and Diana fought daily with Charles trying to convince her that Camilla was just a dear friend and that she was being paranoid. This disgraceful lie found its way down to the lower levels of her royal servants and they branded Diana as a delusional and hysterical fool. With all of this royal crotch swapping going on it should surprise no one that this naïve twenty-year-old girl who was unfairly dragged into this torrid situation was trying to call off the wedding.

She would continue to muse, confuse and puzzle over how Charles could propose to her and tell her that he loved her when he was clearly in love with another woman. The madness continued as mere days before the wedding as Diana caught Charles on the phone to Camilla pleading his love and devotion. Diana was younger, prettier and drove Camilla into desperate acts of staking her claim resulting in many hideous fights. In the end, Diana would plan the fairytale wedding suffering from bulimia, insomnia and severe depression.

When the wedding day finally arrived, it was marked by the United Kingdom having a national holiday as 50 countries and 750 million viewers witnessed a radiant Diana wearing an $18,000 white taffeta grown with a 25-foot train. Charles was dressed in impeccable splendor as he donned his royal military uniform in its full regalia.

On the way to St. Paul's Cathedral for the ceremony the couple's ornate horse drawn carriage rode past 650,000 spectators who lined the streets for a glimpse of the royal couple. Diana looked like a fairy princess straight out of a Walt Disney movie with her radiant smile and alabaster complexion waving to the crowds on both sides of the street.

The Queen and the royal family were taken to the cathedral in eight separate carriages guarded by 4,000 police and 2,200 military officers who were assigned to manage the crowds who were paralyzed in awe at the spectacle that was unfolding. When they finally arrived, they greeted the 3500 guests that were anxiously awaiting their arrival.

After the ceremony the couple greeted 130 guests at the Buckingham Palace reception where the newlyweds kissed on the balcony tantalizing and delighting the crowds that had been gathered below. As if the day's spectacle wasn't extravagant enough, fireworks lit up the night skies for hours to celebrate the historic event as the world joined in the nuptial celebration.

It was indeed a spectacular event that cost, including the distended security detail, a whopping $49 million, but sadly it would be the last day that Princess Diana would spend in happiness as a member of the Royal Family. A few days after the wedding the royal couple took a honeymoon cruise to Gibraltar. The 14-day trip was supposed to kick off their fairytale lives together but shortly into the voyage, Diana's heart would be broken - again.

As the couple opened their diaries to share a combined entry, pictures of Camilla fluttered to the floor. Diana flew into a rage shouting *"why can't you be honest with me? You must always be honest with me!"* Her feelings of abandonment and distrust, which stemmed back to her childhood, compounded the issue as Camilla worked overtime to split their union.

There is no way this situation would end well, and indeed, it did not. The fight lasted several hours and finally subsided the next day when they were having dinner with the Egyptian President, Anwar Sadat, and Diana noticed that two cufflinks had appeared on the prince's wrists.

The engravings on them were two intertwined "C's". When Diana saw them, she pounced on him like a tiger. *"Camilla gave you those didn't she?"* He said: *"Yes, they're a present from a friend."* and that's all it took for the jealousy and fighting to continue. It went on like this for quite some time. Camilla thought it was fun to rub Diana's nose in the fact that she would never be out of the picture, or out of Charles' life, and the head games continued.

From dropping notes to Diana to arrange lunch, to sending bracelets to Charles, to his valet sneaking her into Highgrove (his official residence); It went on, and on, and on. Diana had no rest. Possibly the worst episode was when Diana heard Charles on the telephone in his bathroom saying, *"Whatever happens, I will always love you."*

She burst into tears and Charles discovered that she was listening at the door. Diana was suicidal. The following are Diana's quotes from Andrew Morton's book: *Diana: Her True Story – In Her Own Words:*

"I got terrible, terribly thin and people started commenting, your bones are showing. So that was the October and then we stayed up there [at Balmoral] from August to October. By October I was in a very bad way. I was so depressed, and I was trying to cut my wrists with razor blades."

"It rained and rained and rained and I came down early from Balmoral to seek treatment, not because I hated Balmoral but because I was in such a bad way. Anyway, came down here [London]. All the analysts and psychiatrists you could ever dream of came plodding in trying to sort me out."

"Put me on high doses of Valium and everything else. But then Diana that was still very much there had decided it was just time; patience and adapting were all that were needed. It was me telling them what I needed."

" They were telling me 'pills'! That was going to keep them happy – they could go to bed at night and sleep, knowing the Princess of Wales wasn't going to stab anyone. In those days my greatest pleasure was that I was lucky enough to have a baby on the way. Got married in July and William was on the way by October."

"Then I was told I was pregnant, fine, great excitement; then we went to Wales for three days to do our visit as Princess and Prince of Wales. Boy, oh boy, was that a culture shock in every sense of the world. Wrong clothes, wrong everything, wrong timing, feeling terribly sick, carrying his child, hadn't told the world I was pregnant but looking grey and gaunt and still being sick. Desperately trying to make him proud of me. Made a speech in Welsh."

"He was more nervous than I was. Never got any praise for it. I began to understand that that was absolutely normal. Sick as a parrot, rained the whole time round Wales. It wasn't easy, I cried a lot in the car, saying I couldn't get out, couldn't cope with the crowds. 'Why had they come to see us? Someone help me.' He said: 'You've just got to get out and do it.' I just got out. He tried his hardest and he did really well in that department, got me out and once I was out I was able to do my bit. But it cost me such a lot because I hadn't got the energy because I was being sick with my bulimia – so much; let alone the support for him or vice versa."

"Couldn't sleep, didn't eat, whole world was collapsing around me. Very, very difficult pregnancy indeed. Sick the whole time, bulimia and morning sickness. People tried to put me on pills to stop me from being sick. I refused to risk the child becoming handicapped as a result. So sick, sick, sick, sick, sick."

"And this family never had anybody who's had morning sickness before, so every time at Balmoral, Sandringham or Windsor in my evening dress I had to go out I either fainted or was sick. It was so embarrassing because I didn't know anything because I hadn't read my books, but I knew it was morning sickness because you just do. So I was 'a problem' and they registered Diana as 'a problem'. 'She's different, she's doing everything that we never did. Why? Poor Charles is having such a hard time.' Meanwhile, he decided he couldn't suggest too much."

How these two managed to stay together long enough to have two heirs to the throne was a feat beyond imagination. Nonetheless Charles and Diana kept the public in the dark and their martial charade going long enough to complete their royal duty. Prince William was born in 1982 to a media frenzy.

The royal couple, with their relationship still in tatters, continued to put on the front of happily married royalty before the cameras as they showed the baby to the world. William was a beautiful baby and would go on to become the Duke of Cambridge.

After the birth of William, the relationship between Charles and Camilla, which was ever present, continued to solidify and the love starved Princess decided to go her own way having an affair with a man named James Hewitt.

Hewitt was hired as a horseback riding instructor and became an important figure in Diana's life. In Hewitt, Diana found the compassion and validation that she needed which helped her end her destructive behavior.

He became her confidant and someone that could stand by her while she was navigating the rough waters of her marriage. While the relationship with Hewitt continued, Charles took a royal demand to Diana and Prince Harry was born in 1984 becoming the Duke of Sussex.

Many people have speculated that the red-headed Hewitt was the biological father of Prince Harry and as Harry continues to age, the resemblance between the men is stunning, but Hewitt has repeatedly denied the allegation.

The relationship with Hewitt lasted for five years and when Diana ended it, he attempted suicide. He eventually rebounded trying to sell Diana's many love letters for 10 million pounds. The next love of Diana's life was a man named James Gilbey. Gilbey was a childhood friend of Diana's and at that time, a Lotus car dealer.

The couple were caught on a recorded phone call having an intimate conversation where Gilbey referred to her as "darling" and "Squidgy." To the world the "Squidgygate" scandal was the release of the recorded phone call contents, but to Diana, and those around her, the real controversy was how the conversations were recorded in the first place? Was the palace recording all of her calls? Why?

The scandalous recording, which was leaked by a British intelligence agency, was enough to ignite the press resulting in a fallout that was so devastating to the Princess that she ended the relationship. It is believed that the publication of the tapes accelerated the separation and eventual divorce. Gilbey, a friend of Diana's to the last, has never spoken publicly about their relationship and flatly refused to comment about the matter in any capacity.

The "Squidgygate" transcripts were published in August and by a local tabloid followed in November by the leaked "Camillagate" tapes. The Camilla tapes were an intimate exchange between the Prince and Camilla. The tarnish that the palace would have to endure during this time period was immense.

To make matters worse, people in the UK were starting to take sides. Some supported Diana while others were on the side of Charles. Immediately after the "Camillagate" tapes were leaked, the Queen got involved. She had enough of this nonsense and was putting her foot down to spare the crown from further disgrace.

She arranged a meeting with Charles and Diana and probably felt like clucking their heads together like something you would see in a three stooges' episode. The Queen is very wise and tolerant and has ruled Britain longer than any Monarch in history. She'd been at the helm of the country through the highest points and the lowest depths and when she spoke; mountains moved, and on this day, she was speaking loudly.

The result of that meeting was Prime Minister John Major making an announcement of the couple's "amicable separation" to the House of Commons. With that arrangement the Queen granted both sides their freedom, and now the blame would be squarely placed on them for their extra marital dalliances, and the Royal Family would be spared further embarrassment.

With that, the Queen brushed the unsightliness of the situation from her gloves and moved on. As Diana went about her life, she had a variety of other relationships and flings. Oliver Hoare, an Islamic art dealer and a friend to Prince Charles became involved with Diana after the death of her father. Diana and performing artist Bryan Adams had a romantic fling that burned so hot that he named a hit single after her.

21

She also dated an Army officer, a Rugby player and a man named Theodore J. Forstmann. Forstmann was an investment banker, billionaire and founding partner of Forstmann, Little & Company. Diana was looking for sincerity, understanding, privacy and love, and she was not having the success that she had hoped.

But in all of her flirtations, flings and flubs there was no one that made her heart stop like Hasnat Khan. Khan was a Pakistani cardiologist and heart surgeon that Diana nicknamed "Mr. Wonderful" and their two-year relationship was kept a deep secret.

Khan, a man who was at the very top of his profession, was fearful of the media attention, and the heavy hand of the Royal Family if he was to be discovered as Diana's lover. The relationship grew to be so serious with this very private and caring man, that Diana was introduced to his family under the cover of darkness. Diana was in love and was understanding of his situation but in time grew frustrated.

She wanted to have a life for herself but the pressure that she was putting on Khan proved to be too much. Khan ended the relationship at a late-night meeting leaving Diana in tears. What Diana wanted more than anything was to be loved. Not for her title or her growing fame as an international good will ambassador, but for the little girl that was still trapped inside of her.

2
The Discovery

"Grief is the price we pay for love."

- Queen Elizabeth II.-

Failed relationship, after failed relationship left her a love starved, 36-year-old, single mother or two growing children. As summer blossomed, Diana was extraordinarily sad and in need of an escape. The Princess who wanted to be remembered as the queen of people's hearts, just had hers broken and there was no relief in sight.

Less than a month after the breakup with Khan, in July of 1997, Diana started dating Dodi Fayed. Dodi was the polar opposite of Kahn. He lived a very colorful life in the public eye, and he wasn't afraid of the media spotlight or the potential repercussions of the crown.

He was the son of an Egyptian billionaire named Mohamed Al-Fayed whose business interests included the ownership of Hôtel Ritz in Paris, and two business ventures in London: Harrods Department Store and the Fulham Football Club.

Dodi, then 41 years old, was a Hollywood film producer of the films Chariots of Fire, Breaking Glass, F/X, F/X2, Hook, and The Scarlet Letter. He was also his father's right-hand man at the Hôtel Ritz and fully enjoyed the lavish lifestyle of a global playboy. He had apartments, mansions, helicopters, sports cars, yachts and beautiful women all over the world; and he played with his toys frequently (the lucky bastard).

But with Diana, it was different. Mohamed Al Fayed was a longtime friend of Diana's father and had known her since she was in diapers. After her father's untimely death, he often kept a watchful eye on the family and would eventually employ Diana's stepmother in an executive role at Harrods.

The two families had long and deep respect for each other. Diana first met Dodi when they were children but reconnected in 1985 when Dodi's polo team had a match in Windsor where they played, and defeated, Prince Charles' team. At the match, Dodi and Diana met as the long-lost friends that they were, but like most people who find themselves romantically involved at the midpoint in their lives, they both had baggage.

Diana was still carrying strong feelings for her former love interest of two years, Hasnat Kahn, and Dodi was engaged to be married to an American model and actress named Kelly Fisher. While Diana's relationship was already over, Dodi's was, apparently, in full swing. In fact, the month prior to his involvement with the Princess, Dodi and Kelly had purchased a home together in anticipation of their wedded bliss.

The romance between the Princess and heir to the billionaire's throne began quickly. So quickly in fact that the when Dodi hastily ended the engagement to Kelly Fisher, she swiftly hired an attorney and filed a breach of contract suit against him for $440,000 in Santa Monica Superior Court. As it turns out, Fisher wouldn't be the only one who would be shocked by the relationship.

After accepting an invitation by Dodi's family for a seven-day Mediterranean holiday, Diana's mind started racing about what the future might hold. On the morning of July 11th 1997, one of Muhammad Al Fayed's helicopters was sent to Kensington Palace.

Within minutes Diana, her two children and their luggage were collected, and they were flying to France where they boarded Harrod's executive jet. From there the threesome boarded a tender boat which delivered them to Jonical, Al Fayed's 20-million-dollar luxury yacht which then set sail to his St Tropez mansion.

As she relaxed in the sun, she began crafting her future. The holiday in the company of old friends and a benevolent Egyptian billionaire who was loathed by the British establishment, fulfilled everything that her heart desired. Dodi was worldly, well mannered, attentive, and wrapped in his father's wealth.

Diana, always desperate to escape the paparazzi (when she wasn't manipulating them) stayed in the guest quarters of Al-Fayed's thirty room villa where her boys made good use of the sprawling private beach and many jet skis.

It was the perfect place for the Princess to unwind but she would never be far away from the paparazzi's camera lens. Their photos of the couple sent the tabloids into fits of wild speculation. After seven days of fun in the sun, the newly formed couple departed to tend to their responsibilities.

A week later, Dodi, after finishing his business transactions in Paris, returned to London to visit the Princess and take her to Paris for a weekend getaway to his Imperial Suite at the Ritz Hotel. It was at this point that the Royal Family, who already monitored and tallied her every move, fully understood the gravity of their relationship.

As the Crown rolled both their eyes, and their stomachs; the couple's private vacation on board Jonical set sail to Corsica and Sardinia with the paparazzi in hot pursuit. One of the tabloid photographers named, Mario Brenna, grabbed the opportunity take a photo of the couple kissing on its deck.

The now famous, and infamous, photograph which will forever be called 'the Kiss' sold for 1 million pounds (the equivalent of $1,240,300.00 in today's money) and drove the world wild with speculation. Immediately after the photo was taken, the couple went looking at engagement rings at Alberto Repossi's jewelry store in Monte Carlo.

This is, and always has been, a topic of debate but one thing is certain, the couple was inseparable. The next day they returned to London and spent the evening at Dodi's apartment where their obligations sent them in different directions. Diana traveled to Bosnia to gain world exposure for her International Campaign to Ban Landmines (ICBL).

She wanted to add to the 100 countries that were already prominent supporters of her cause. Her visit lasted for three days where she met with, and consoled, victims who sustained dreadful injuries from mines planted during the country's savage civil war.

Immediately upon her return, a Harrod's helicopter picked her up and delivered her to Mohamed Al Fayed's house in Oxted, Surrey. She spent the following day with Dodi, relaxing at their 600-acre estate, while Mohamed visited his in-laws in Finland. This jaunt ended with the couple returning to London.

As they rose the next morning the story of their relationship broke in The Daily Mirror, confirming the veracity of the earlier rumors that had become more than whispers throughout Buckingham Palace. The color photo of their kiss while they were aboard Jonical, days prior, was sprawled on the front cover creating the shock factor that everyone at the newspaper had hoped for.

Diana's reaction was quickly decoded by her friends, including her butler and closest confidante, Paul Burrell. Below he recalls his conversation with Diana about this self-made media buzz in the documentary entitled *Diana: The Royal Truth.*

Burrell: *"Have you seen Hasnat?"*

Diana: *"Yes, I went for a drink with him last night."*

Burrell: *"What does he think about your being here in South of France with Dodi Al-Fayed?"*

Diana: *"Well, he's not too pleased."*

Burrell: *"Has he seen the pictures in the papers?"*

Diana: *"Yes, he has because you know his routine. You know, every morning he goes to the corner shop and sees the press."*

Burrell: *"You know that, and I know that's what you are doing. You are manipulating the world's media by having these pictures taken to show Hasnat who you are with. It is sort of a, are you jealous? Do you mind? Do you care? Are you bothered?"*

"That's what Diana was saying to Hasnat Khan through those pictures in the world's media, and, of course, until Hasnat was bothered, and I didn't find out recently that he called her the day before she died on her mobile phone. He called her to try and patch up their relationship. Had she returned to London, I truly believe the romance between Hasnat Khan and the Princess would have been rekindled. It was too strong. It was too deep. They were true soulmates."

Unfortunately, timing was not on their side and as the relationship with Dodi quickly progressed, Hasnat slowly melted into obscurity. The man that she once called "Mr. Wonderful" was no more. Diana was ready for the next step in her life and wanted to be a bride, something that Hasnat, who wanted to live a very private life, wasn't ready for. Soon after the story broke the couple flew to France where they boarded Jonical for another cruise in the picture-perfect Mediterranean.

Speculation swirled that the fast blooming relationship, now known the world over, might be more than just a summer fling, and if that were the case, the possibility that Diana might marry Dodi and leave the country was a real one.

On Friday, August 29th, Jonical was anchored in the sparkling waters off Carla di Volpe, a private Sardinian resort when Dodi made the decision to fly to Paris. The couple arrived at 3:30 in the afternoon staying overnight at Dodi's apartment. The plan was to spend the next 24 hours in Paris before returning to London.

The jarring reality that gripped the whole of Britain was that the 20-year-old virgin bride had now outgrown the bonds of the Prince Charles, the Royal Family, and the pettiness of their island. In the same way that a butterfly abandons a cocoon, Diana had evolved to show the world her new colors. She was now the most photographed woman in the world, an international superstar, and an emerging goodwill ambassador for her many causes.

Sixteen years after her marriage, she starting to listen to the advice of her sons. They had both been urging her to live abroad to increase her privacy and it looked as though they were going to get their wish, but in the words of the 18th century Scottish poet, Robert Burns, *"The best laid plans of mice and men often go awry."*

It was now the morning of August 31st, 1997 and it was to be Princess Diana's last mortal day on earth. Her day began as she sipped tea with Dodi aboard his yacht. The two were admiring the gorgeous Emerald Coast of Sardinia as they laughed, held hands and planned their day.

After a time, they decided to board Dodi's jet and fly to France to spend some time in Paris. Dodi knew that he could easily sell her that story, because she loved Paris, but his sole purpose for going there was to collect the engagement ring that he had ordered weeks earlier.

The big day had finally arrived, and he was planning to propose marriage. When the jet landed in France there was no fanfare. No one alerted the airport that a VIP flight had arrived and there were no special instructions from the French or the British governments. The only people that were present and accounted for were the paparazzi. As usual they were tipped off by their paid plants within Dodi's security group.

When Dodi saw the photographers, he was less than pleased, and he knew their faces well. They were the same crew that could be counted on to poke their lenses in every facet of the couple's life. Dodi was usually a pretty good sport about the paparazzi. He understood that they needed to make a living, but what they didn't understand, was that this trip was going to be very special and the couple's privacy wasn't requested - it was demanded.

As Trevor Rees Jones led the couple down the stairs of the jet, he explains what he saw. The following is an excerpt from his book, The Bodyguard Story: *"As Diana appeared, their engines started up. The tensions between the Princess and her pursuers that had built up, like the heat, over the summer were ready to boil over. Ordered by the Ritz, two vehicles, a Mercedes and a Range Rover, waited at the bottom of the ramp with their drivers." "*

One was Philippe Dourneau, Dodi's regular driver and a licensed chauffeur of Etoile Limousine, the other, Henri Paul , a thinning-haired fortyish man with glasses, was the assistant head of the security for the Ritz. Dodi walked directly up to him, shook hands and chatted. Trevor had met him before. ' But he didn't click with me as a person. He was perhaps a little too chatty... but obviously Dodi had lots of faith in the man, the way he went to speak to him straight off.'"

They quickly packed the couple, their luggage and their staff into their cars and raced off to Mohamed Al Fayed's Villa Windsor. There they walked the grounds of their future home for forty-five minutes and then the couple drove to the Ritz. As the bodyguards moved their luggage into the hotel's Imperial Suite, Diana had her hair done in the beauty salon while Dodi drove the Mercedes the few hundred feet to the Repossi jewelry store to collect Diana's engagement ring.

The couple rested before their dinner reservation and Diana used the time to call her sons who were vacationing with Prince Charles in Scotland. She then called journalist Richard Kay informing him that she would be withdrawing from public life by the end of the year. It would be the last call she would ever make.

Minutes later the couple were chauffeured across town to a restaurant named Chez Benoit, but Dodi decided that it would be too crowded for him to propose marriage, so they circled back to the Ritz. Finally, the two-car convoy arrived at the front entrance of the hotel which was a circus of photographers.

The princess impatiently waited in the car for the crowd to be managed and glanced at her watch, it was 9:55 pm, and the night was droning on far longer than it should have. Finally, they were cleared by their security detail to safely exit the Mercedes and they quickly scurried into the lobby being bathed in photographers' flashes.

As they covered their faces and put their hands in front of the paparazzi's camera lenses, they bolted directly up to the Imperial Suite where they could finally escape the madness. Still trying to shake the paparazzi so the couple could have a peaceful ending to their holiday, Dodi devised a last-minute plan. He decided to send a decoy car with his regular chauffeur, Philippe Dourneau, and his back up driver to the front entrance of the hotel which would be very visible to the paparazzi.

Meanwhile, Henri Paul, would escort the couple out the back door where they would slip away in a separate car undetected. At 12:05 am Dodi's personal security detail were becoming frantic and start racing toward the back door of the hotel looking for the driver of the second car, Henri Paul. Their pulses were racing because they know that if the timing wasn't perfect, the two-car plan would never work.

They were soon met by Dodi and Diana leaving the Imperial Suite and then finally by Henri Paul returning from his decoy show at the front door. The foursome hustled into the black Mercedes S-280 and began to cruise way. Their destination was Dodi's apartment on the Rue Arsène Houssaye and it was a route that the paparazzi knew well.

Henri Paul was driving with Trevor Rees Jones in the front passenger seat. Behind Paul sat Dodi and to his right, and behind the front passenger seat was Princess Diana. It was 12:09 am on August 31st, 1997 and the plan to escape the attention of the photographers worked flawlessly.

As the car raced away from the Ritz to Dodi's apartment on the Rue Arsène Houssaye their Mercedes entered Pont de l'Alma tunnel with a swarm of paparazzi on motorcycles in hot pursuit. At a high rate of speed, the car swerved as it passed a small white car on its driver side, clipping its left taillight. This impact caused the Mercedes to violently weave back and forth and finally to lose control veering to its extreme left crashing full force into the tunnels thirteenth support pillar.

This impact created a large "V" shaped indent in the front of the car which folded the bumper, grill and the entire front assembly into the engine. The result of the tremendous impact with the concrete pillar caused the car to recoil and spin immediately to the extreme right, finally coming to rest, facing the opposite direction and in the opposite lane.

The impact pushed the engine and transmission back through the firewall and the steering column into the driver, Henri Paul. As the steering wheel impacted his chest it crushed his rib cage and ruptured his vital organs. The driver never had a chance and was killed instantly. Dodi Al-Fayed, who was seated directly behind the driver, received the full brunt of the impact plus the driver's weight back into his chest killing him instantly as well.

Trevor Rees Jones' survived, but nearly three quarters of his face was completely torn from his skull upon impact with the windshield. He bravely tried to exit the vehicle, but the impact from the crash jammed his door preventing it from opening. As he lay semi-conscious and bleeding from his face in extreme pain, he could hear Diana moaning behind him.

Diana's crushed body was jolted into an awkward position on the floor of the car, trapped between the rear framework of the front seat and the back-seat cushion. Incredibly, the white car was only slightly damaged from the sideswipe with the Mercedes and nonchalantly turned to the left passing the crushed vehicle without impedance or concern.

As bitter of an irony as you will ever find, the same photographers that they were so desperately trying to avoid were on the scene taking endless photographs of those who desperately needed help. When the authorities arrived, they had to physically remove the paparazzi as they were impeding those trying to give aid to the victims.

When help did arrive, they found Trevor Rees Jones' in dire need of medical attention. Diana was semi-conscience with blood streaming from her face as she writhed and moaned in pain calling for Dodi to help her. She mumbled to those attending to her *"Oh my God, what's happened?"*

As they lay trapped in the twisted wreckage of what was once a fine automobile, all four bodies were tended to by the emergency personnel that had arrived. They quickly took control of the scene loading Diana and Trevor into separate ambulances and started administering treatment to their wounds.

The paparazzi were quickly rounded up by the police for questioning and all of their film and camera equipment were impounded for evidence. Each were separately strip searched, questioned and their testimony recorded. As the world slowly became aware of the identity of the crash victims, Diana's ambulance stopped multiple times to attend to her devastating cardiac issues while enroute to Pitié-Salpêtrière hospital.

Their attempts were in vain as she was declared dead on arrival at 5:57 am. Within minutes the phone rang in London summoning Prince Charles, Diana's sisters and other members of the Royal Family, to Paris. Their task was to pay their respects and accompany Diana's body back to London.

Diana's death was a full-blown media spectacle in constant search of a villain. The first reports were that the paparazzi had hounded the car causing it to swerve and crash. When members of the paparazzi were released by the French police without being charged, the blame then switched to the driver of the mysterious little white car who witnesses claimed had intentionally sideswiped the Mercedes.

By the traces left at the crash scene the car was identified as a white Fiat Uno. Authorities conducted a nationwide search for the car resulting in no useful evidence, then results of the autopsies began pouring in. Accompanying Britain's intense mourning, a mourning so great that it shut down the entire country, were newspapers and tabloids that were cranking out various explanations of the crash, and a sea of flowers that had been lovingly placed at Kensington Palace.

The conduct of the British people was impeccable on this day as they showed the world the respect and grief that they had for the queen of people's hearts that would never see the throne. The royal family stood frozen in place without a comment, statement or an answer for the outpouring of affection that they were witnessing.

In their wildest dreams they would have never expected the impact that Diana had on their loyal subjects or how she touched their emotions in way that no member of the royal family ever had - before, or since. The only normalcy that could be observed was the flag over Buckingham Palace flying at full mast indicating that the queen was in residence there, but beneath the royal standard their family had no idea what to do.

They knew that discontentment was growing around them and that were unsure how to handle it. After all, Diana was no longer a member of the Royal Family and had been stripped of her official title. In what capacity should they acknowledge her?

During this time there was a tremendous amount of pressure on the Royal Family which ended on the 5th of September as the Queen appeared on television to make a 3-minute public address. Queen Elizabeth had guided her nation through horrors that would have crippled most leaders, and her words of solace were the perfect elixir to soothe the grief-stricken masses.

As mourners stood vigil their mood retreated into an eerie and somber calmness as they slowly came to grips with what was about to transpire. In the predawn hours people began pouring into London to mourn the loss of a woman who struck a chord in their hearts and to position themselves at vantage points along the funeral route ten rows deep. It was a day that no one wanted to see but everyone felt that it was their duty to attend.

The sun rose to greet a heavy fog that hung in the air so thick that it made your hair moist with fine droplets of dew. There was a solemn feel almost as if the universe knew that this was the day that Princess Diana would be laid to eternal rest. As the sun rose higher in the sky it cascaded down upon the crowds as they patiently and obediently managed their growing anticipation.

At 9:08 am the bell of Westminster Abbey broke the deafening silence of the mourners whose hushed whispering rolled down the pavement for miles. The tolling bell signaled Diana's funeral cortège to leave Kensington Palace and begin her final journey. Her casket was lovingly draped with the royal standard which was fitted to perfection as the ermine border flowed on its perimeter.

Placed on top of the royal garment were three wreathes of large white lilies which added to the gravity of the spectacle. The casket was gently lifted onto a gun carriage that was slowly pulled by the six horses of the king's troop.

In front of the cortège were two rows of mounted Metropolitan Police officers whose horses stepped in unison. The procession was followed by six Guardsmen impeccably dressed in scarlet colored uniforms that were accompanied by Welsh Guards in full military dress and regalia.

As the cortège passed the mourners that had been waiting for hours along the streets they cried, wailed and threw flowers. Although the British are known as a country famed for keeping a stiff upper lip, their loyal subjects openly wept, and in some instances were overcome with spasms of uncontrollable grief.

Finally, the little girl who had such a sad upbringing, marriage and divorce was getting the outpouring of love and respect that she was due, but sadly, she would never see it. The funeral was televised around the world and was watched by more than 2 billion people, but shortly after Diana's burial, everyone's grief turned to rage; and someone needed to be held responsible. Within days the toxicology report of the driver, Henri Paul, revealed that he was under the influence of a combination of alcohol and prescription drugs while he was operating the vehicle, and with that release of information, the final villain (and scapegoat) was found.

The mainstream media knows that people will repeat any parochial story that is fed to them, so they constructed this version of the official fiction describing what caused her death.

To the collective glee of their media gatekeepers, this nonsense has been parroted around the world for decades resulting in the quiet acceptance of the masses who are living their lives like a hope chest with a broken lock.

This version of Diana's death is the equivalent of saying that the Kennedy assassination happened because President Kennedy was just playing with a rifle and it suddenly went off. It has always amazed me how mankind will walk upright, with his eyes wide open, right into the abyss of his own making.

There were many questions that were left both unasked, and unanswered, and in the next chapter we will address them - all of them. Do not despair that you have been lied to. Darkness, true darkness, isn't the absence of light, it's the absence of hope.

3
The Questions

"I don't go by the rule book; I lead from the heart, not the head."

- Diana, Princess of Wales -

Now that the elementary history lesson of the first two chapters is behind us, it's time to start digging and separate the myth from the reality. Anyone who has read the first three volumes in my *Who Murdered?* book series fully understands that widely repeated stories can be taken as the truth, when they really aren't true at all.

This is a tactic used by the global media cabal to trick stupid people into doing the bidding of their masters. Human beings are a trusting lot, and they automatically assume that if every television station that they watch is telling them the same story or bombarding them with the same message then it must be true.

Unfortunately, all of those television networks are run by the same major corporations who share the same belief system and they are trying, desperately trying, to get you to believe their brand of bullshit. This vast propaganda takeover began in 1996 when US President Bill Clinton signed the Telecommunications Act which deregulated media and promoted media cross-ownership.

Prior to that, there were thousands of independent media companies, all of which had their own opinions, voices, and investigative reporters. Shortly after the Telecommunications Act was signed, the huge media conglomerates bought as many of the little smaller media companies that they could get their hands on so they could completely control everything that you see, read, and think.

How else do you think that the same "catch phrase" can be repeated on different networks, on the same day, and at the same time? Whether their battle cry of the day is "defund the police" or "Russian collusion"; it has all been designed for you to absorb, and the more vicious the message gets, the more desperate they are trying to get you to believe it.

Yes, folks, you're being totally controlled and brainwashed. That might be why so many of the early television network logos used something that resembled an eye, a spiral, or a bullseye; but I'll save that for another book - someday.

The global media cabal is well aware that you will believe and repeat a story if it comes from your friends faster than you would if it came from lying political leaders that we pay to roam the hallowed halls of our pillared government buildings. This is why so many friendships, relationships and even marriages have died a slow death at the hands of the media's sociological penetration.

In short, the media's very job in the 21st century is to radicalize the overly trusting, naïve, and well, just plain stupid, to get them to spread their propaganda messages for them – and you know what? It works like a charm. Don't we all know people like this? Artificial experts who are nothing more than media canaries?

Today critical thinking, the art of asking the right questions, and forming your own opinion that is different than what your friends have been told to think has become a lost art. When I was in college, they taught you to think – not *what* to think, and it makes me sick to see people being spoon-fed nonsense and swallowing it without the slightest bit of objectivity.

To me, this "rolling over on command", is beyond tolerance and in early September of 1997, immediately after Diana's funeral, the bereaved citizens of Britain, and their counterparts in France, agreed with me. Eventually their sorrow would turn to anger and then to rage, as they simply didn't believe what they were told. Eventually even members of the mainstream media began asking questions about the oddities surrounding Diana's death.

Their questions were not the of conspiracy theories or half crazed people; these were legitimate questions that begged to be asked, that no one seemed to have answers to. During my investigation I have added clarity to these nagging questions by dividing them into two categories.

The first category, which seems to be where the majority of everyone's attention was, and still is when they try to investigate her death and produce solid answers, are smaller questions. They're so small in fact that I have named them "micro questions." This category was quickly populated by the investigations, inquests and media inquiries that followed.

None of these questions will ever solve this elaborate puzzle or produce the solid answers necessary to find a smoking gun. The micro list has been combed over for decades producing nothing of real worth, and certainly nothing that would satisfy everyone's battle cry for justice.

There were literally dozens of these questions to sift through, which only lead to more questions, that no one, by design, has answers to. The most pivotal of these questions have been reduced to the following. I call this list my top ten.

Why wasn't Diana wearing her seat belt when it was routine for her to do so? The night of the crash Diana was not wearing her safety belt and was out much later in the evening than was normal for her.

Her friend, confidante and butler, Paul Burrell, has illuminated these questions claiming that the Princess was normally tucked in bed much earlier in the evening and was far more cautious in automobiles. Evidence shows that the Princess had been frightened by brake failure while she was driving her Audi in 1995.

Why was the driver going at such a high rate of speed? This is another open-ended question that no inquest or investigation has been able to solve. Beyond the over modulated claim that the driver was intoxicated at the time of the crash, no has been able to add any clarity to this question, but if Henri Paul was drunk, and I said if, because the evidence points to the contrary; he would have driven at a snail's pace. Law enforcement officers would be the first to tell you that highly intoxicated drivers operate their vehicles at a very low rate of speed, not a fast one.

Why did they clean up the crash site so quickly? This is another subject of great debate that no one seems to have an answer to. Whether you are investigating a traffic accident or a homicide, investigators preserve the site until all of the necessary evidence has been gathered. Rushing to re-open the tunnel, at 3am, and then calling in a specialized van to spray the entire tunnel down with high pressured hoses, makes no sense.

Why were the security cameras turned off on the night of the crash? The closest logical explanation that I have heard was that due to the privacy laws in France, cameras can only be pointed at buildings or private property, not at public streets. This is an explanation that falls flat on its face when you can clearly see that cameras have been installed by the government and that they are pointing at the street, presumably for a reason.

How was the drivers blood alcohol content so high when he didn't appear drunk on camera? For me, the obvious answer is that he wasn't drunk at all. People who swiftly walk up and down stairs and bend down to tie their shoes without having an issue aren't intoxicated to the high level suggested in the toxicology report.

Much like the film that surfaced after the Warren Commission Report in the Kennedy assassination that showed the bullet coming from a different direction then they claimed; the film footage of Henri Paul wasn't seen before they made their fabricated media campaign. This won't fit their narrative; but Henri Paul was as sober as a judge.

Why did it take so long to get Diana to a hospital? The official fiction claims that they had to stop several times to attend to the Princess as she was going into cardiac arrest. This make absolutely no sense unless they were shorthanded and needed the driver to assist in their life saving efforts. Why they waited until the very last minute to remove Diana from the wreckage is a question that no one on the planet has an answer for as the rear of the car was intact.

Why was the car at the rear door of the hotel not under the supervision of their security team? Of all of the questions, this one haunts me the most. If the security team at the Ritz had done their job and properly secured the vehicle, the rear entrance, or the personnel; Diana would be alive today. The fact that using that entrance was an afterthought is they only excuse for these security gaps and that will be discussed later in the book.

Who was driving the white Fiat Uno that clipped the Mercedes? Of all of the elements to this murder, this has been the one that has been researched, pondered and argued over the most. Entire books authored by very seasoned researchers have been written on this aspect of the crash, and I believe that all of them have it wrong. This is the tiniest component of this murder but the only one that left actual physical evidence behind, thus the analysis paralysis.

Why did the French police gather eyewitness testimony and then ignore it? The French authorities gathered and used only the testimony that they were told to use in order to fit the media narrative that they were going to promote. The rest of the witness testimony was either discarded, suppressed or lost.

Why have the witnesses to the crash been threatened? This is one of the best questions that has ever been asked and no one in authority, in any country, has the answer. To date, at least seven witnesses have either been assaulted by mysterious people or have had their lives threatened. To finish this question. I'll ask another, who is doing the threatening?

These are the same nagging questions that have been asked by people great and small in every county around the world since the impact of the Mercedes on August 31st, 1997. So why are people so interested in the micro list and not in digging further and asking the bigger questions? I believe the answer is simple. They really don't want to know. Enter the term, "Normalcy Bias" and its ugly definition: "The phenomenon of disbelieving one's situation when faced with grave and imminent danger."

Applied to this case, if you don't dig for something, you won't find it, and won't have to react or change your life over it. The truth about Diana's death would be so traumatic that you couldn't handle it, so you don't seek it. It's far easier to ask small questions that are easy to digest like; "was Diana engaged?" But the title of this book is *Who Murdered Diana?* and that's exactly what I will reveal to you.

While everyone seems to be obsessively focused on the 10 questions that I have previously listed, no one is examining the bigger questions that must enter this investigation on the all-important second category called macro questions.

Answering the macro questions will outline the suspects that we will run through the process of motive, means and opportunity in the next chapter. There are only five macro questions that I have come up with that have somehow eluded everyone.

Who hated the Princess?

Who wanted her dead?

Why did they want her dead?

Who cooperated in the coverup?

Who profited from the murder?

It was at this point in the investigation that I started to strip my mental gears and could only come up with one conclusion. Either Princess Diana was a victim of a pre-planned and pre-meditated murder, or this is the wildest stroke of bad luck and misfortune ever recorded in the annals of human history.

To fully grasp the situation, now decades past the event, you must fully understand who Diana was in the 1990's and the global influence that she wielded. She thrived in a time before social media, Netflix or even the 24-hour news cycle. Back then, you had a handful of television channels and everyone's attention was on one woman.

She looked like a centerfold whose regal stature, grace, and connection to one of the most wealthy and powerful governments in the world garnered the attention of every television network, magazine and power broker.

When she scheduled a press conference, or attached herself to a humanitarian cause, the world stopped and listened. She was one of the most powerful women on earth who could get Presidents, Prime Ministers and even dictators to bend to her will and support the causes that she attached herself to.

Unfortunately, as readers of my other books have learned, anytime someone of immense power pulls public opinion away from the desires of world leaders, that person always dies – in a suspicious way. Diana would be no different.

She was an unstoppable force in bringing attention to her favorite humanitarian causes such as the elimination and removal of landmines and aiding those suffering from HIV/ AIDS and Leprosy.

But as she championed each of these causes and put pressure on the world leaders for change, the world's defense contractors, arms brokers, bankers, and pharmaceutical companies began to loath her and they wanted her to shut up.

What she was proposing may have made sense in the humanitarian world but if she got her way it would have cost major corporations billions and billions of dollars. These were serious perils that she was simply too naive to comprehend.

Each time she spoke of her causes, she created an outcry putting pressure on very powerful people behind the scenes, and in some cases, even making them look foolish. These were very powerful people that you simply don't want as your enemies.

While managing to manipulate the world's biggest media networks to her every whim with her charisma and good looks, she was also making fools of the Royal family. While her intentions of helping people were genuine, there was also an underlying motive of making Prince Charles eat his heart out in envy of what he'd lost and to make him look like a fool for leaving her.

Adding to this were her visits to greet commoners with handshakes and hugs. Her continued visits to Britain's sick and indigent, did not set well with the queen. Not only was she leaning on the nerves of the world's arms brokers and pharmaceutical companies, she was also making the standoffish and overly stiff Royal family look ridiculous for not being as warm and inviting as she was.

Ironically the same altruism that made her the shining star to her fans around the world by vowing to transform the British monarchy, and trying to rid the world of weapons and disease; were the same causes that brought about her murder.

So, we must ask ourselves, who had enough global juice to murder Diana and get two of the world's oldest countries to cooperate with each other on the cover up? After all, the French and the English had a checkered past to say the very least. Below is a short list of conflicts between the two countries.

Anglo-French War (1109–1113)
Anglo-French War (1116–1119)
Anglo-French War (1123–1135)
Anglo-French War (1158–1189)
Anglo-French War (1193–1199)
Anglo-French War (1202–1204)
Anglo-French War (1213–14)
First Barons War (1215–1217)
Poitou War (1224)
Saintonge War (1242–43)
Guyenne War (1294–1303)
War of Saint-Sardos (1324)

Hundred Years' War (1337–1453)
Anglo-French War (1496–1498)
Anglo-French War (1512–1514)
Anglo-French War (1522–1526)
Anglo-French War (1542–1546)
Anglo-French War (1557–1559)
Huguenot rebellions (1627–1629)
Anglo-French War (1666–67)
Nine Years' War (1689–1697)
Queen Anne's War (1702–1713)
King George's War (1744–1748)
Carnatic Wars (1746–1763)
Seven Years' War (1756–1763)
Anglo-French War (1778–1783)
Anglo-French War (1793–1802)
Napoleonic Wars (1803–1815)
Anglo-Vichy French War (1940–42)

These conflicts resulted in possibly the biggest losing streak of any country in world history. Of the twenty-nine conflicts and wars between the two countries the English won all but one of them, and while the most recent period of history has resulted in a newfound tolerance of each other, this is a streak that hasn't been forgotten by the French. So, who could have pulled such a string to gain the multi-generational cooperation of two of the oldest enemies in world history?

Answering this question, alone, broke the case wide open and began to answer the micro and macro questions listed in the beginning of the chapter. But before we get to that, let's take a look into the level of cooperation that existed between the English and the French during this investigation.

We all know that the initial reports blamed the driver of the car, Henri Paul, who was allegedly driving at a high rate of speed and under the influence of alcohol, trying desperately to avoid tabloid photographers who were in hot pursuit. Alright, fine, that part of the story, which later fell apart under closer scrutiny, seemed to be logical enough on the surface.

But what happened after the crash could only be likened to outtakes of a Marx Brother's movie. Witnesses were gathered by the French Police for interrogation and their testimony was lost, not one time, dozens of times.

The multiple doctors who were already in the tunnel, and had witnessed the crash, showed up at the scene and were not allowed to help. The Ambulance who treated Diana, paid more attention to removing the dead bodies than trying to help the Princess. This is hardly the immediate attention that you would expect the most famous woman in the world to receive.

When she was finally removed from the car and was placed in the Ambulance she was moaning, talking and conscious. But the Ambulance turned out to be more of a hearse than an emergency medical unit. There were numerous hospitals that were equipped to handle a situation such as this, but the Ambulance team debated on which facility to take her to.

When they finally decided to take her to a hospital, a mere four miles away, it takes another 15 minutes for the hospital to agree to receive her. For the hospital to agree? Ponder that for a moment. Isn't tending to the sick and injured a hospital's job? How are these delays possible?

The complete incompetence of the ambulance team took Diana, a woman of royal blood in France and of royal marriage in Britain, on a casual low speed, almost leisurely drive to the hospital. A drive in which they stopped and fiddled with her numerous times most likely aggravating her condition.

When the Princess finally arrived at the hospital it was 2:07 am, nearly two hours after the crash. Take a moment to comprehend that. It took them two hours to drive four miles. That's unimaginable because people run "the four-minute mile." Diana would have been better off ordering a Domino's pizza, who guarantees 30-minute delivery, and back riding to the hospital with the delivery guy.

Dodi's father, who had his own issues with the British government over his ownership of Harrod's and who was repeatedly denied English citizenship for private (yet unknown reasons) was highly suspicious of the crash and immediately started a self-funded multi-year investigation of the events.

He insisted that Diana and Dodi were killed to prevent the royal family from being "polluted" by his Muslim bloodline and began a campaign to prove Diana's crash was a plot to murder her.

Incredibly, Diana, before her death, had complied several threatening letters that she had received and personally handed them to Dodi's father. He took the papers, carefully examined them, and put them in his lockbox for safe keeping. Diana then told him that if anything happened to her that the Royal Family and MI6 would be responsible.

The detailed documents were threats that she had received over the last 18 months as she knew that her life was in grave danger. In his mind, this car accident, was no "accident" and he found himself agreeing with Diana that Britain's M16 spy agency was behind the assassination, but he needed to be sure.

Within two months Al-Fayed hired John MacNamara to conduct a private investigation into the crash while embracing the public probe by the French police that was headed by Herve Stephan. MacNamara was colorful character. He was already employed by Mohamed Al-Fayed as his Chief of Security for Harrod's Department Store and was a retired

Metropolitan Detective Chief Superintendent and a retired veteran detective from Scotland Yard. His impressive background as a law enforcement officer and his loyalty to the Al-Fayed family made him the obvious choice for the job.

Mohamed Al-Fayed was furious and wanted answers, and to date, no one has invested more time and treasure to produce it. In the end he would spend in excess of 13 million dollars investigating the crash and the motives that led up to it, but his conclusions were far different than official fiction produced by the dual investigations of the French and British governments in the Paget Report.

This report was the end result of Operation Paget which was spawned by the British Metropolitan Police inquiry in 2004. The true purpose of this elongated investigation was to refute the evidence that had been uncovered and widely publicized by Al-Fayed's investigative team.

The 832 page report was promoted as a document that was assembled in painstaking detail by automobile accident experts and fourteen experienced police investigators which cost £12.5 million, a figure that was more than £10 million over its original budget.

In the end, The Paget Report was nothing more than an elongated damage control document designed to tell one side of the story using only the supporting facts that its contributors selected for you to see.

Our handlers, who are comprised of our governments and other powerful figurers of authority, don't openly lie to us unless there is something worth lying about. In the next chapter we will establish the "persons of Interest" associated with this case and figure out why everyone is trying so desperately to protect them. Soon, you will know, without a doubt, who murdered Princess Diana.

4
The Suspects

---

*"I clearly heard the warning: 'You never know when an
accident is going to happen.' (Diana) went very pale."*

- Simone Simmons, Diana - The Last Word -

Before we get into the pushing and shoving of
who did what, it's important to understand the process
that we must undertake to find the murderer.

When a crime is investigated, facts are gathered
in an attempt to find those responsible so they can be
brought before the courts and due process of the law
can determine either their innocence or guilt.

That's how the American criminal justice system
functions – at least in theory. When the facts are
examined, criminal investigators put their personal
feelings aside and follow the flow of the evidence to
individuals who are called persons of interest.

A person of interest is a phrase used by law
enforcement to announce the name of a person
involved in their investigation but who has not been
formally accused or charged with a crime.

In reality, a person of interest could be a witness,
bystander, or someone that law enforcement speaks
with for the purpose of conducting their official
investigation. From there, detectives can screen and

58

sift through witnesses and other persons of interest to find their suspects, and eventually make their arrests. This isn't an easy process, or a process based on speed – it's a process based on the methodical gathering and examination of facts. This exacting process outlines three elements for finding a suspect. The three elements are motive, means, and opportunity.

Each suspect must have, within the findings of the crime, the motive, the means, and the opportunity to achieve the given result. This three-element theory has proven to be so successful that it's now the primary foundation of crime-solving. According to a popular online dictionary, the definition for each of these terms are as follows:

Motive: something (as a need or desire) that causes a person to act.

Means: the medium, method or instrument used to obtain a result.

Opportunity: a favorable juncture of circumstances causing an action.

In the murder of Princess Diana there were numerous persons of interest who should have been questioned if indeed an unbiased investigation into her suspicious death had transpired. In leu of an honest investigation the world got a show trial that was remotely controlled from behind the scenes.

Certainly Mohamad Al-Fayed, his family, Diana's family, and almost everyone else on the planet would have welcomed such an investigation, but instead of law enforcement officials and investigators actually doing their job, they produced a one-sided document designed to pacify the press, their governments and their paymasters.

This not only seems strange, but it borders on illegal, as all of these factions were working in concert to perform these acts. In any court, in any country, that is the very definition of a conspiracy.

Two questions arise at this point that must be answered. Why was it done and who was behind it? After all, people don't go to such elaborate and coordinated extremes without a reason or a motivation.

Answering the first question of why it was done seems to have a straightforward answer. They wanted to trick as many people as possible into being silent, obedient and to swallow their story.

Those who continued to ask questions beyond the official fiction would be discredited as conspiracy theorists and labeled as crackpots. Give the wide-eyed and naive population something to swallow to gain their obedience and discredit those who question and disagree with the other side of the story.

It's a fairly simple tactic which happens to work extremely well. With that established, we must move on to answer the second, and I believe the most important question, who was behind it? To answer these questions, we must first ask many others and delve into the first of the three elements of a crime: Motive. After all, people just don't kill other people without a motive, so that is the logical place to start. It's also important to keep in mind that the motive of a crime is the trickiest of the three elements.

Some motives generate fury, while other motives are simple disappointments that eventually dissolve within a person and become lost over time. Knowing this, it's important that we analyze each suspect closely to determine the root, and intensity behind his or her motive.

The following process is repeated in every book in my series to reveal the murderer. In the case of Princess Diana, there were numerous people at high levels who had an 'axe to grind'. After an exhaustive period of research, I have compiled the following list of potential aggressors who had the motive to commit murder.

1. The Royal Family

2. The Paparazzi

3. Kelly Fisher

4. Kasnat Kahn

5. Arms Brokers

6. The Pharmaceutical Industry

I. MOTIVE

Motive: something (as a need or desire) that causes a person to act

The Royal Family

There are so many reasons that members of the Royal Family wanted Diana dead that it would be impossible for anyone, anywhere, to count them all, but beyond question, top on their list was the bombshell interview that she gave to BBC journalist Martin Bashir.

The 1995 Panorama TV interview was her first solo interview since her wedding and 22.9 million viewers watched as she constantly lampooned her husband, Prince Charles, as well as the crown.

During the course of the interview she told the world about Charles' longstanding infidelity, his insensitivity, her mental suffering, her eating disorder and her opinion that Prince Charles didn't have the desire or the ability to become the future king.

She further embarrassed the Royal Family by claiming that the monarchy was losing its relevance and needed to be modernized. She also said that *"I would like a monarchy that has more contact with its people"* which was a comment that certainly didn't land well.

Throughout the next several years, after her divorce, she went on a crusade of compassion laden causes which up-staged the crown and her former husband further illustrating her comments.

The Royal Family was furious and wasn't about to take the publicized airing of their dirty laundry lightly, nor would they be lectured about their rules, customs, or traditions.

The monarchy has always held itself to a very high standard in the public eye and to risk that was threatening the continuation of the respect level of the institution itself. Diana's rogue and defiant nature was an insult that was so inflammatory that something needed to be done about it.

The interview was the last straw for the royal marriage resulting in the Queen insisting that they immediately divorce. For the purposes of fulfilling the element of motive to kill, there is no need to go any further. Of the laundry list for things that would follow, this pissed the Royal Family off the most, but was it enough for them to plan her murder?

The Paparazzi

Diana had a bittersweet relationship with the Paparazzi. With one phone call or even the slightest mention of an event, cause or public appearance that she could possibly attend, she could garner the entire world's attention which she would bend to her every whim.

In short, that much attention made her the most influential woman in the world who was able to take her message above the heads of world governments and directly to the people.

Candid photos of Diana in any uncompromising position could be vended to any number of the major news outlets for inclusion in their publications and could bring millions of dollars of profit for the photographer who was lucky enough to supply them.

This meant that wherever she went, she would be hounded relentlessly by the Paparazzi who were all hoping to cash in on her image to receive a financial windfall.

This created an enormous amount of pressure on the Paparazzi as the welfare of entire families relied the images that they could harvest. Did someone pay the Paparazzi to cause an accident to get the most lucrative and exclusive photographs in history?

Kelly Fisher

Kelly Fisher is an American model who had met Dodi in Paris in July of 1996. In February of 1997 after an intense love affair he gave her a $180,000 engagement ring and bought her a $5 million home in Malibu, California where they would start a new life together.

He convinced her to quit her lucrative profession as an underwear model and receive a $2,000 a day allowance. Kelly Fisher was on her way to wedded bliss with one of the most promising young film producers in Hollywood, but the engagement wouldn't last.

An ABC News article from April 14, 2009 entitled *Did Dodi Two-Time Diana?* states the following: *"Dodi Fayed had all-night sex sessions with his previous girlfriend Kelly Fisher at the same time he was seducing Princess Diana in the Mediterranean, according to transcripts of phone calls between Fisher and Fayed released at the Royal Courts of Justice yesterday.*

"You even flew me down to St. Tropez," American underwear model Fisher told Fayed, "to sit on a boat while you seduced Diana all day and fucked me all night." The blunt telephone conversation was recorded, according to Fisher, in August 1997, just weeks before Princess Diana and Dodi Fayed, the son of the owner of Harrods, died in Paris in a car crash."

August 9th 1997 was a day that Kelly Fisher will never forget. That was not only the day that she was supposed to wed Dodi, but it ended up being the day that she was dumped by him during a telephone call and the day that Dodi's relationship with Diana first hit the newspapers.

In short, August 9th, 1997 was the day that Kelly Fisher's life collapsed. The next day was supposed to be the first day of her new life with Dodi, but instead, she woke up to see photographs of Diana and Dodi plastered in every media venue.

By the 14th of August Kelly's heartache turned to rage and then to revenge. The teary-eyed model was now back in Malibu appearing on television with her attorney showing the world a gigantic engagement ring that Dodi had purchased for her.

At the widely publicized press conference, her attorney announced plans to sue Dodi Fayed for *"emotionally leaving her at the altar"* when he began his romance with the Princess. Kelly Fisher was indeed a scorned woman, but was her scorn deep seated enough to murder Dodi and his new love interest?

Kasnat Kahn

Of all of the men that Diana had been involved with, Kasnat Kahn was the man that completely stole her heart. Kahn was a sweet and gentle man who was a Cardiologist by trade. The two met at the Royal Brompton Hospital in London were Diana was visiting a friend who was recovering from a heart operation.

In Kahn, Diana found the emotional availability that she frequently needed as her rows with the crown and her public persona intensified. Diana's butler, Paul Burell, recalls having to sneak Kahn into Kensington Palace under the cover of night so that they could spend some time together away from the prying eyes of the Royals and the press. Finally, after two years of hidden romance, Diana, put pressure on him to take the relationship public. From Diana's perspective, that seemed to be a logical progression, but Kahn wanted nothing to do with the attention from the media or the Royal Family that would certainly follow any such announcement.

He saw the way that Diana had been constantly badgered by everyone with a camera and he knew that she would forever put his profession, as well as his privacy, in jeopardy. Finally, Diana gave him the inevitable ultimatum. Either advance the relationship in public or we must split.

This was the precursor to the relationship with Dodi and the famous photographs of them together on his yacht. Many of Diana's close friends, including her butler, have stated that she was actually using Dodi to put on a show. She desperately wanted Kahn to see them together and come running back to her, but did it backfire? Could the jealously that Kahn felt be a motive to murder Diana?

Arms Brokers

Those who knew Diana best know that nothing was as near and dear to her heart as her numerous causes for the betterment of humanity. She was indeed one of the kindest, sweetest, and most angelic public figures that the world has ever known.

Of her many humanitarian efforts, none was closer to her heart than her campaign to end the use of landmines in every country around the world. In July of 1996, a full year before she began her relationship with Dodi, she announced her support and involvement in a global anti-landmine campaign.

After working many months behind the scenes, she decided to show the world the level of personal injury that these weapons were inflicting. To accomplish this, she summoned the worlds media to cover her visit to the war-torn region of Angola.

After a successful trip there, she set her sights on a three-day trip to Bosnia to press the same message there. By the 18th of August, a mere 13 days before her death, US President, Bill Clinton, along with 100 other nations, announced that they would sign a global anti-landmine treaty.

Consider that timeline while remembering that trillions of dollars are made each year on the manufacture and sale of munitions and landmines in both legal and illegal venues.

By creating such a campaign, Diana found herself at odds with powerful people in many countries. While this hurt their pocketbook, was it enough to create a motive to have her murdered?

The Pharmaceutical Industry

In 1987, at the peak of the world's HIV / AIDS hysteria, Diana met the virus head on. During that time, the promoted medical fact was that those infected with the terrible virus could transmit it through casual person to person contact.

In April of that year Diana headed to the opening of Britain's first AIDS ward at the Middlesex Hospital in London. There she appeared in photographs, which would eventually make the front page of newspapers around the world. The images showed Diana shaking hands with those infected with the virus without the protection of rubber gloves or a facemask.

This was not the only time that she appeared in such a fashion. Over the next several years as she traveled the world holding infected infants which melted away the promoted fears of the medical community.

This contact was taboo and ran contrary to the promoted medical wisdom of the time. The rumors that this deadly disease that was easily transmitted through human contact was started and promoted by the medical community and their boardroom partners in crime, big pharma.

With Diana embracing the victims and showing them unprotected compassion, it removed the hysteria of the virus reducing the blood money potential that the medical community was banking on. If you want to sell a pharmaceutical product at a high price/profit, you need a few elements. 1) global need 2) global fear and

3) global urgency. Diana's publicity of unprotected contact was killing the cash cow that they had worked so hard to fatten with their well-oiled propaganda machine that was spoon fed to the world's media.

Needless to say, she enraged both communities who stood to make gigantic profits from what she was exposing. This threatened trillions of dollars in profits that could be made selling truckloads of vaccines to terrified governments who were all begging to pay.

Summary of Motives

Clearly, each suspect or group of suspects had a clear-cut motive to murder Diana with the exception of the group that the world media tried to convince everyone was guilty of the deed – the Paparazzi.

Beyond question the Paparazzi behaved badly when they arrived on the accident scene as they snapped hundreds of photographs of the victims, including that of a semi- conscious Diana in the backseat.

But beyond that, they had no motive to murder Diana. Why? The answer is simple, a dead Diana meant the end of their cash flow. It would be impossible to sell candid photos of Diana to any press outlet or periodical with her dead, and that runs contrary to their best interest.

Therefore, the Paparazzi had no motive to murder Diana and must be dropped from the investigation. As we proceed to the second element of a crime, the establishment of means, the field will continue to narrow.

II. Means

Means: the medium, method, or instrument used to obtain a result.

I hate that definition because I think it makes things overly complicated. Having the "means" to commit a murder is really just fancy term for having a way to do it. For example, I may want to steal the crown jewels and I may have all the motive in the world, but without a way to do it - it can't be done.

The same thing applies here, and that's where examining "means" comes into play. In order to solve the murder of Princess Diana we need to examine each of the suspects according their "means". Let's examine the remaining suspect list . . .

The Royal Family

Kelly Fisher

Kasnat Kahn

Arms Brokers

The Pharmaceutical Industry

The Royal Family

Did the Royal Family have the means to be in Paris the night of Diana's crash and/or plan her murder? Britain is not only filled with some of the most loyal, kindest and toughest people; they are one of the oldest, wealthiest and most powerful countries in the world.

Simply put, this is a country that is not to be taken lightly, underestimated or trifled with. If you piss off the Brits you will awaken a beehive of resolve and pay a tremendous price for your misdeeds.

This is a lesson that Adolph Hitler learned the hard way as he bombed their densely populated cities for 57 consecutive nights during World War II trying to force the British people to surrender or at least bend to his will.

He greatly underestimated the spirit of their people, and the mental toughness of my 6th cousin, Sir Winston Churchill. A firsthand account of these bombings is covered in an in-depth interview in my book *Who Murdered FDR?*.

There, my 94-year-old aunt, who was living between Birmingham and Coventry during the bombings, and who worked to build the famed English planes, the Spitfires, gives a firsthand account of the daily suffering that they endured.

Germany, like the French before them, suffered massive military defeats by the emboldened British whose mastery of the seas and far reaching intelligence networks could garner the crown virtually anything they wanted.

Beyond any question, doubt or level of uncertainty, the British government, with their well-established spy and intelligence networks entrenched in every country in the world, could certainly have had their MI6 or MI5 operatives in Paris on the night of August 31st, 1997.

Especially, when you consider that the British and American governments frequently share intelligence between them and work hand in hand on operations involving their security on a national level.

Kelly Fisher

Although Kelly had all the motive in the world to seek revenge on Dodi, and probably Diana as well, for crushing her dreams of marital bliss, she couldn't have carried out this level of revenge.

Not only would it have been virtually impossible for her to mastermind and carryout a murder on such an international level, but it would have been an even greater stretch for her to have constructed the elaborate coverup that soon accompanied it.

Further, she wouldn't have had the intelligence operatives in place to know where or at what time the accident would have taken place. Aside from the victims in the fatal car accident, Kelly Fisher was the most victimized person on the planet in this situation and was probably the most innocent victim of circumstance.

Hasnat Kahn

Although it was not his way to show it, Hasnat was in love with Diana, and according to her Butler, Paul Burrell, the reverse was also true. While Diana's pet name for Hasnat was "Mr. Wonderful", their two-year relationship ended in June of 1997. Burrell said in an interview that Diana was trying to make Hasnat jealous by posing with public photographs with Dodi onboard Jonikal and that she was trying to persuade him to tip his hand.

I have been placed in that situation over the years by more than a few girlfriends and the rage always ends up being waged against the guy that was planted to make the scheme happen.

I suspect that this was also the case with Mr. Kahn and there was some evidence to suggest that this middle school tactic was actually starting to work as he did attempt to reach out to her. I have no doubt that Hasnat had a jealous reaction toward both Diana and

Dodi, but like Kelly Fisher, he couldn't have carried out the murder to even the score, even if he was the sort of man to do so. He couldn't have masterminded and carried out a murder on an international level, he didn't have the intelligence operatives in place to know when or where the crash was to happen, nor could he have constructed the elaborate coverup that accompanied it.

Arms Brokers

Diana's campaign against landmines not only rocked world governments, their allies and their global agendas, but it also rocked the international arms brokers and the defense contractors who supplied them en masse. In many respects the money that is passed through the hands of the arms brokers and manufacturers is a lion's share of a government's yearly budget and they wield substantial power both within individual governments and throughout their global network of allies. These arms brokers and defense contractors share governmental intel and can reach out and touch you wherever you are. They definitely had the means to murder Diana.

The Pharmaceutical Industry

The drug companies within the Pharmaceutical Industry who were working on treatments and vaccines were both happy and unhappy with Diana. They were happy with her because she was raising awareness of AIDS / HIV, Leprosy, and other illnesses that the governments were flooding money into to discover broad-based treatments. They were unhappy with her because she was shedding light on governmental woes that some very powerful people wanted to keep low key. Any group that works hand in glove with governmental agencies has access to their operatives, especially when there are billions of dollars on the line. Beyond question the Pharmaceutical Industry had the means to murder Diana anywhere in the world that she visited.

Summary of Means

Having neither the means or the opportunity to murder, both Kelly Fisher and Hasnat Kahn must be dropped from the investigation. Even if they had the motive to murder, they didn't have the means to carry out their revenge.

Also dropped from the investigation is the Pharmaceutical Industry. Despite having the motive and the means to carry out the murder, they were already being paid handsomely by world governments to conduct clinical trials.

According to the NIH (National Institute of Allergy and Infectious Disease), the first HIV vaccine clinical trial was opened at their Clinical Center in Bethesda, Maryland in 1987. 1988 saw the first successful phase 1 trials and by 1992 they were well into the Phase 2 trials.

While the Princess didn't do them any favors as the awareness that she raised harmed their cause originally, she broadened the worlds desire for the necessary help that the vaccine would supply. As we move into the third and final stage of the investigation, opportunity, only the Royal Family and the Arms Brokers remain.

III. Opportunity

Opportunity: a favorable juncture of circumstances causing an action

The Royal Family

Beyond any doubt the Royal Family, with the capabilities of MI5 and MI6 at their disposal, could position operatives to carry out any task, in any country that threatened the Monarchy.

In fact, you would be hard pressed to find anyone better in the intelligence community than the two agencies of MI5 and MI6. Even other world agencies, of equal skill, have great admiration for the British and their network of operatives.

Arms Brokers

With billions, if not trillions, of dollars at stake in the mix of governmental dealings and international conflict, international Arm Brokers not only have the operatives to carry out any task, in any country that threatened their wealth, they also had the cooperation of the governmental intelligence agencies that they are working with to supply them with whatever inside information that was necessary for them to murder.

SUMMARY OF OPPORTUNITY

The Royal Family and international arms brokers have now satisfied all three elements of a crime and have been successfully transformed from mere persons of interest into full blown murder suspects. It is now becoming clear, that someone in the employ of these people either acted alone, or in concert with one another, to murder Princess Diana.

EXAMINING THE SUSPECTS

All good investigators have one thing in common: they ignore their personal likes and dislikes and follow the evidence connecting the dots to solve the crime. This was a major stumbling block for many investigators, especially those in the UK, because they were emotionally attached to the outcome.

As loyal British subjects they would have either had an affection for the Royal Family and their rule, or a level of distain for the Royal Family over their treatment of the Princess. In short, the Royal Family is and always has been their central focus.

For me, being an American investigator, I am seeing things through different eyes which is allowing me a certain level of objectivity. In short, while I have great respect for Britain and the Royal Family, I do not obsess over them. In my investigation they are nothing more than a murder suspect to be examined and their evidence calculated.

The two biggest spy networks in the world are owned by the British and the American governments, and both had been watching, listening to, and calculating Diana's every telephone conversation, private affair and public appearance with great intent for the last three years of her life.

While it remains unclear whether the British enlisted the help of the Americans, or they were both equally enamored with the Princess at the same time, the cold hard facts now state, very clearly, that they were both spying.

Also being looped into the spying intelligence fray was the government of France. While they were not surveilling Diana to the extent that the British and the Americans were, they were certainly privy to all of the information that was being gathered.

The Russian intelligence machine was also being informed of Diana's actions through their highly placed double agents within these agencies. But why? What could this woman have possibly done to attract the full attention of these elongated spy networks and why was the information being distributed so widely between these governments?

The answer was influence. Because Diana had the rare ability to take her message directly to people and bypass the policies of each individual government, she had the ability to create a coup d'état in every government that she visited and she was making the world's power brokers very nervous.

Her agenda didn't align with theirs, and they weren't at all happy about it. To a lesser extent the FBI and the CIA had seen this before. My book *Who Murdered Elvis?* explains in great detail why the United States government got so heavily involved drafting Muhammad Ali and Elvis Presley into the armed forces at the peak of their careers.

Elvis and Ali, who would go on to become very good friends, were influencing the population in a direction that the American government disapproved of. Elvis was gyrating and grinding his hips on stage which insulted, offended, and infuriated the conservative American public so much that they were mailing letters to the FBI demanding that they do something.

Soon death threats started pouring in and the same FBI that was called on to remove Elvis from society were being called to aid in his protection. Because Elvis was negatively impacting society and they knew that he wasn't a serious threat to national security, drafting him into military service to let everything calm down was their best option.

This same formula was repeated nearly a decade later when Muhammad Ali, who had converted to a black Muslim faith that had close ties to the Black Panthers and other militant groups, began protesting the war in Vietnam. When Ali refused induction into the armed forces, it emboldened the large protests of the Vietnam War that became so common during that time period.

To answer the call governmental operatives infiltrated their supporters and murdered Malcom X. That was a shot across the bow of their cause that promised more to come as Ali was stripped of his boxing license, passport, and his title.

But when it comes to the king of American agitators one must stand in awe of John Lennon whose FBI file is the thickest and most comprehensive file I have ever seen. Lennon's file had to have taken thousands of hours to gather and compile because he was not only very vocal against the war in Vietnam, but he wasn't an American citizen.

The FBI and other cooperating agencies labeled him a dangerous foreign revolutionary that was constantly under the influence of psychedelic drugs and who was trying to influence the 1972 American Presidential election.

Their greatest fear was that he would stage a national propaganda concert tour that registered the youth of America to vote against Nixon and his pro-war policies. Their answer to this menace was to put the FBI on the task of nailing him on a narcotics charge that would get him deported and solve their problems.

That resulted in a four-year legal battle with him being denied permanent residency in the United States. After the election, Lennon took a hiatus from music to raise his son, Sean. When he restarted his career, he was murdered in the most mysterious of ways.

In each case, the subject's popularity led the American citizens away from the desires of their masters; this was the case with Princess Diana, but with her, things were a little different. Her massive appeal and popularity weren't just influencing the opinion of one country, it was influencing every country in the world, and the people who really ran the world, knew that she needed to be stopped.

This explains who organized her murder, but it doesn't explain why. To fully understand the gravity of their motives we have to examine all of the aspects of the second murder suspect, international arms dealers.

Arms dealers, arms brokers and arms manufacturers work hand in hand with the nations of the world and have access to their intel on international military conflicts which impact their orders, supply chain and ultimately their profit margins.

In 1997, the biggest arms manufacturers in the world were the United States, Britain and France, the same countries that were heavily engaged in spying on Diana. Why? As we've already discussed, at the time of her death her primary focus had been promoting global legislation of an anti-personnel landmine campaign that was going to cost them billions of dollars in lost revenue, and worse, were the rumors that landmines were just going to be the beginning of her anti-arms campaigns.

After the landmine campaign Diana was going to start a global campaign which would ban small arms and after that, who knew what would be next? When the intel of these three nations heard this, you knew that heads were going to roll. No one wanted to kill Diana, and they did everything possible to avoid it. At first, they tried to warn her, hoping that would make her abandon her meddling.

The first warning came publicly in the form of a newspaper article shortly after her trip to Angola in January 1997. Earl Howe, a British government junior defense minister, was quoted in *The Times* saying that Diana was *"ill-advised and is not being helpful or realistic… We do not need a loose cannon like her."*

Following suit was a comment by Peter Viggers, a Conservative politician and Member of Parliament, saying that Diana's efforts didn't *"actually add much to the sum of human knowledge."*

Weeks later a more private threat was delivered. In February of 1997, six months before her death, Britain's Armed Forces Minister, Nicholas Soams, phoned the Princess in Kensington Palace. Diana who was with her friend Simone Simmons summoned her to the phone so she could hear what he was saying.

The following quote is from the Paget Report on Page 109 and it was never seen by the jury *"The Princess of Wales apparently beckoned Simone Simmons to the telephone and they placed their ears to the receiver. Simone Simmons heard a male say, 'Don't meddle in things that you know nothing about, because you know accidents can happen'. She stated there was an inflection in the voice which both she and the Princess of Wales found threatening."*

The rest of the account is covered on page 75 in the book by Simone Simmons and Ingrid Seward entitled Diana -The Last Word. *"I heard a voice telling her she should stop meddling with things she didn't understand or know anything about, and spent several minutes trying to tell her to drop her (anti-landmines) campaign. Diana didn't say much, she just listened, and I clearly heard the warning: 'You never know when an accident is going to happen.' (Diana) went very pale."*

" *The moment she put the phone down we started talking about what he had said. I tried to be reassuring which was not easy – she was clearly very worried. She told me that she wasn't going to be put off, but that after that call she felt that it was vital to take precautions. She gave me and her friend Elsa Bowker a copy of the Profiting Out of Misery dossier. I took it home and hid it at the head of my bed under the mattress protector.*"

According to Simmons, the dossier was authored by Diana and included the names of influential people including members of the Secret Intelligence Service that Diana believed were behind the sale of British landmines. Diana was about to have the dossier published telling Simmons that if anything happened to her, the murderers would be MI5 or MI6.

Simmons said she had hidden the dossier, along with various other documents that the princess had given to her for safe keeping, but after Diana's murder she made the wise decision to burn them saying. "*. . if they could bump Diana off, then they could bump anyone off – and I value my life.*"

Apparently what Diana didn't understand was that she wasn't just ruffling the feathers of MI5 and MI6; she was interfering with the economies of every nation on earth who profited from the sale of landmines, munitions, and other arms deals. That is what cost Princess Diana her life.

5
The Rabbit Hole

"You could say all the elements that led to her death were just a tragic coincidence but part of me believes it could have been six months in the making. While I was working in Angola earlier that year we had lots of meetings to discuss ways Diana might be killed or injured.

- Alan McGregor, Diana's bodyguard , The Sun-

The Royal Family turned the other cheek and tried to ignore Diana's public tirade. Their ultimate hope was that she would eventually get it out of her system, remarry, and move out of the UK taking whatever angst that remained with her.

Although they were certainly not thrilled with her, they had everything to lose and nothing to gain by her murder. The Royal Family obeys rules, very old rules, that demand that they behave in a manner of conduct that is both superior to, and far above that of their loyal subjects.

To put themselves in harm's way by doing anything that would cast them in a negative light would put in jeopardy their very existence and the future of their monarchy. This is something that they certainly wouldn't risk as their primary focus is the longevity of their bloodline and maintaining their pious image.

They also had a greater understanding of how the world worked and they knew that Diana would eventually be killed before her dossier could be published, but they also knew that it wasn't in their best interest to bother with it.

They certainly weren't happy with her, and the feeling was quite mutual; but they wouldn't be the one to silence her, but they certainly knew she would be silenced. The wisdom and patience of the Royal Family paid off as the intelligence trio of the American, British, and French agencies were sharing anything and everything with the arms brokers as they have for decades.

It was normal operating procedure for those who profited from the blood money associated with the manufacture and sale of weapons. By the time the summer of 1997 rolled around the only thing left for them to do was to decide on the location of her assassination and who would do it.

This riddle would be solved in the most public, and also the most private place on earth; the annual Bilderberg Conference. The Bilderberg Conference gets its name from the hotel where the first conference took place in the spring of 1954 and hosts roughly 150 members of the European and North American political, financial, industrial, and military elite.

The location, date and agenda of the meeting are always different, and it is always widely publicized because of the high-profile cast of global characters that are invited; but the meeting itself is always held in private.

Needless to say, security for these events, which can be held anywhere in the world, is extremely tight. In fact, the security for one the meetings in the not so distant past, was handled by Airbus; the biggest arms manufacturer / military defense company in the world.

This conference itself is like any conference that you would attend with one key exception. It assembles the most powerful players in every industry and is designed to bypass the voters in their countries. In these meetings the elite can discuss and alter world policy as they see fit without the will, knowledge, or input from their citizens.

These are the people who really rule the world regardless of who is running for political office and comedian George Carlin said it best. *"It's a big club, and you ain't in it. You and I are not in the big club."* In 1997, the "Big Club" was having their 45th conference on June 12-15 at a lake resort near Atlanta, Georgia.

At this particular conference the attendees, whose guest list read like a list of Gods from Britain, France and the United States, were welcomed by Hillary Clinton with a publicized agenda of discussing NATO, China, Islam, EMU (Economic and Monetary Union of the European Union), Energy, Growth and Corporate Governance.

All of these noble subjects were freely discussed as the media had widely publicized, but at night when the liquor started to flow among very powerful friends the discussions turned into a tawdry tirades and gripes, and whose name was on everyone's lips? None other than their number one obstruction, Princess Diana.

This, and other information, came to me in spring of 2020 during the height of the worldwide covid19 hysteria. As the world was shut down, a person from a little town in France contacted me through a popular social media outlet. Through one of my posts they were made aware that I was in the throes of writing a book on the murder of Diana, and they sent me a private message.

They wrote that their mother, who had been investigating the death of Diana for more than fifteen years, had recently died, and they wanted to pass her information onto me because it needed to come out. At this point, my book was already written and only weeks away from being published.

They asked for my mailing address so they could send me a packet and I was tempted to say that I didn't it want it, because I knew what it meant. It meant that I would have to completely rewrite my manuscript which was already three months overdue. Being both skeptical and suspicious of this contact, I gave them the address of a local post office box, and eleven days later, a thick legal sized envelope appeared.

In it was 371 pages of information on Diana's death. Oddly the envelope had no name or return address on it, and when I went to recontact them via social media to confirm the delivery; the user had vanished. It took more than a week to read through their packet and digest the information, which was no easy task, but in the end, it reinforced my conclusions.

Beyond question Diana was standing in the way of not only the untold fortunes of the arms dealers, but of the international politics that they were trying to exploit. What intrigued me most was how they described a private meeting that occurred at the Bilderberg Conference long after the day's activities had ended.

As the night wore on and the bottles of the finest booze that could be found anywhere on earth began to empty, the crowds began to grow thinner and thinner, until only the most determined and most devious among them remained.

By 2 am the liquor-soaked factions had settled deep into their private talks that had given way to discussing their most private of concerns. Among them were a group of three men nicely tucked away in a corner. They sat facing each other in hip-high burgundy leather lounge chairs that were lined with shiny brass studs.

They were strategically placed around a lacquered wooden coffee table whose dark color seemed to glisten in the dimly lit environment and added the perfect ambiance to their sinister talk.

The scene was couched by luxurious marron patterned carpeting and in the background, the walls were muted by a thick velvet corrugated curtain that overlaid the dark brown wooden panels.

By now the joy of their annual reunion had lost its allure and was replaced by the concern that was etched on their faces. One was a global financier; another was an executive of an arms manufacturer and the third man was a politician with substantial ties to the UN.

They sat with their legs crossed and their drinks welded to their hands as they bobbed their highly polished wingtips. Now in their sixteenth hour their expensive business suits, that were pressed to perfection at the beginning of the day, were creased and rumpled.

Their neckties were loosened and pulled down to the middle of their chests to allow the partial comfort needed to continue their meeting. The men were entering their second hour of conversation when it was overheard.

The financier: *"Has anyone had any luck trying to scare the Princess off?"*

The arms executive: *"No, a few people in her circle have hinted that she needs to stop, but it had no effect. I know that someone called her on the telephone and made it clear to her that she was way in over her head and that accidents can happen. They thought that certainly she would catch the hint and move on, but again, she wouldn't drop it. They've tried to discredit her in the media to make her look like a fool but that didn't work because the Royal Family had a fit. They said it made them look bad, because everyone thought they were behind it, but they weren't."*

The politician: *"well we can't have her out there running around the international community pushing this ridiculous weapons ban and shaming everyone to sign it. It's political and financial suicide. I don't know what we're going to do but this can't go on."*

A very long and awkward pause came over the men as they continued toward the bottom of their whiskey glasses. Finally, one of them said *"Political and financial suicide? Maybe that's exactly the answer."*

The arms executive said with a laugh, *"you mean get her to commit suicide? Well that certainly would solve everyone's problem wouldn't it?"*

The politician: *"No, that's not what I meant, if she won't stop her crusade, then she needs to be stopped."*

The financier quickly butted into the exchange: *"Are you suggesting that we have the Princess killed? Have you completely lost your mind?!"*

The arms executive: *"I know the people that can make that happen, and it's not their first time."*

The financier became irate and slammed his glass on the coffee table with such force that ice cubes jumped out of his glass and danced around the top of the table. He quickly stood up and said *"I can't believe that you two are actually considering this. You're both crazy and I want nothing to do with this. As far as I'm concerned this conversation never happened."*

As he turned to quickly walk away his eyes locked with the person that would become the source of my information and he paused momentarily. Almost as if he said to himself *"oh shit!"* then he quickly composed himself and bolted out of the room.

The conversation between the men continued with the Politician saying: *"you certainly have all of the intel that you need to find the right place and make it look like and accident, but we can't have any witnesses and we need an Oswald, you know, someone to hang it on. If she doesn't start getting a lower profile, that's an option."*

The two men remained in the conversation but were startled by the abrupt exit of the financier. They also became painfully aware that they were within earshot of other people and apparently had been the entire time. One of them said, *"It's almost 3:30, let's talk about this in the morning."*

Nothing more was heard of Diana during the rest of the conference which ended as formally as it began, and the two men were never seen again. But who were these men? If my source is to be believed, one of them, who he called the financier, was Gianni Agnelli. Agnelli who held the title of an Italian Industrialist was indeed one of the most powerful and wealthiest men in the world.

He was not only head of Fiat corporation, he also controlled 4% of Italy's GDP and was directly involved with worldwide military manufacturing and their contracts. Two things were known of Agnelli on this day, he was a member of the Bilderberg steering committee who invited the members to the meeting, and he wanted no part of any conversation that involved bringing harm to the Princess.

Another man in the trio, was a portly man with a beefy face, who was later identified as Samuel Berger. Berger, also known as Sandy Berger, was named on the Bilderberg participant list as "Assistant to the President for Security Affairs."

That title was as downplayed as it could possibly get as Berger was a governmental genius for the United States. He held many storied positions throughout his career, but at that time, he was officially a Deputy Assistant to the President for National Security Affairs for President Clinton.

That position placed him as a chairman of the Deputies Committee of the National Security Council and a sub-cabinet interagency group in charge of the coordination of foreign policy. The third man in the conversation was unable to be identified but he was tall and gaunt with brown hair and he spoke with a very thick French accent.

Diana ignored the warnings that had been given to her and three days after the Bilderberg Conference had ended, she came to Washington, again pressing her international ban on anti-personnel land mines.

Roxanne Roberts of the Washington Post quotes her as saying *"My purpose was to draw world attention to this vital but hitherto largely neglected issue." "Anyone would be drawn to this human tragedy and therefore I hope you will understand why I wanted to play my part in working towards a worldwide ban on these weapons."*

The article continues *"Each month 800 people are killed and 1,200 others are maimed by stepping on mines. More than 70 countries, led by Canada, support a permanent ban on the weapons, but the Clinton administration does not, nor does China, Russia or India. Diana is trying to change that."*

She ended her visit by walking hand-in-hand through the streets of the Bronx with Mother Teresa and then met President Clinton and the First Lady at the White House. The purpose of her White House visit was obvious, to pressure the Clinton administration into signing a landmine ban that they genuinely had no interest in.

By July, Diana, who was now merging the worlds of glamour model, fashion icon, rock star, missionary, humanitarian, and potential saint; appeared on the cover of Vanity Fair magazine. In the article she was telling the world how she was coping with her divorce and rebuilding her life.

By now many people realized that the motivation behind her star power was to show Prince Charles what he was missing and rub his nose in her fame and good works. On August 9th, after more subtle hints and a few stern warnings by establishment leaders and their minions; she traveled to Sarajevo, the capital of Bosnia, where she continued to raise public awareness for her landmine ban.

Her three-day visit was widely publicized by the BBC where she visited the homes of landmine victims and greeted others in their rehabilitation centers. Diana's global influence was so great that only nine days after her trip to Bosnia, US President Bill Clinton publicly announced his agreement to sign her anti-landmine treaty.

As the international community and their pollical leaders financially groaned over how far her arms ban would go, and what her future bans might be, they started to find themselves at odds with those who supplied their arms. In the past they had always worked together swimmingly but Diana, whose gorgeous looks and growing charitable star power, was straining their relationship.

The leaders of these governments were being publicly shamed by Diana into signing her landmine ban at one end, but at the other end, that was fracturing their agreements with their arms manufacturers and crippling their economies. Interfering with the money source from high profile people with shadowy figures in the background is no place for Mary Poppins.

It was impossible for this situation to end well; and indeed, it did not. A mere 46 days after the Bilderberg Conference drew to a close, the most glamorous and photographed woman in the world was dead, and of the most suspicious of circumstances.

As with all sudden fatalities of mega stars, everyone was searching for information and there was none to be found. Everything by design, was tightly held. Immediately following the crash the French police ignored several eye witness accounts who tried to explain that there were motorcycles and a small white car that were working in concert to disorient the driver and push the car into the concrete barrier that caused the horrific crash.

A transcript of the video by Timeline entitled, *Diana: The Night She Died,* features the interview of one crucial witness that was directly behind the Mercedes and was ignored by the French Police as he did everything in his power to give his account. His name is Eric Petel and the translation of his completely ignored account is shocking.

Petel's account was translated from French. he speaks. . . *"I started to go down the curve I saw headlights blinking. The car was going quite fast and then I hear as the car's running, an implosion. I thought my exhaust was the trouble, but I heard this implosion."* *"As I'd just bought my motorbike, I thought it made the noise. So what do I do? I slow down and check if my bike's gone funny and then I hear a loud boom - the car crashing."*

As he approaches the car to help, he notices a woman in the back seat. He continues with his account. *"I get hold of the person in the back, she'd fallen against the back of the passenger seat in front and was bent over the seat in front and I start to move her back. Then, at that moment her head flops back, I see blood coming out of her ear and coming out of her nose. And I say to myself that's weird I know this person."*

But Petel's night of horror didn't end there. In his attempt to summon help for those who were injured in the car, he sprinted to the closest phone box and rang the emergency services. Knowing the gravity of what he had just witnessed, he then ran to the nearest police station.

When he arrived, he was out of breath, and badly shaken as he tried to give his eyewitness account to the officers; officers who had no interest in what he was saying. Petel continues; *"I threw some files on the floor, so they got more police to try to calm me. The more they tried to calm me the more upset I got and what they did was put me in handcuffs. So they got another officer to deal with me." "And then a very senior officer - I won't give his name - he simply said it would be best if I did not make myself known. It felt very much like a threat. I didn't know who it was [involved in the accident] then."*

So why is it that the French police didn't listen to him? Could they have been fed knowledge of the assassination? We may never know, but what is clear by Petel's interview was that they first ignored him, then they claimed that he was not telling the truth and finally they said that he wasn't speaking clearly enough.

If we chose to dismiss Eric Petel's account of the accident, as the French police have, do we also ignore the testimony given by Clive Goravoodoo? David Crawford, an attorney for Trevor Rees Jones, recounts Mr. Goravoodoo's comments.

"[he] was on the bridge above the l'Alma tunnel, he and also was a chauffeur and he was his car was parked and he was waiting for the people he was waiting for to come out of their restaurant or cinema or something and he was having a cigarette on the bridge over the l'Alma tunnel and he heard this- this car coming towards him and he heard a very loud noise, and he-his conclusion I think was that the person driving that

car had actually engaged neutral and then pressed the accelerator. That was the sound of a racing engine not in gear which he described."

Petel and Goravoodoo weren't the only witnesses to be ignored and then threatened. American tourists Jack and Robin Firestone were vacationing in Paris with their son at the time of the crash and were in a taxi being driven in the opposite direction in the tunnel.

They witnessed the moments after the crash in the opposite lane through the wide spaces between concrete pillars as traffic slowed to a crawl. They told their stories to the French Police, who were completely uninterested.

I had the luxury of being introduced to Jack Firestone through a mutual contact and spoke with about my investigation. He would go on to tell me that not only did the French Police ignore their statements, they were also ignored by the British inquest that followed. When they pressed the issue, they were given the answer that their statements had been "lost" - for more than ten years.

Unfortunately, the threats to the Firestone family over the years have caused them to change their address, phone numbers and email addresses frequently. Just when you thought that there would be no one left to be threatened for witnessing this "accident" you'd be wrong.

According to a 2008 article by CNN entitled "*Bodyguard threatened after Diana's death*" Trevor Reese Jones, the only surviving member of the crash also was threatened. The article quotes "*He sustained serious injuries in the August 31, 1997 crash and testified that he received anonymous phone calls and letters after the accident, threatening him to keep quiet. He said the caller told him to keep quiet, saying, "We know who you are, we know where you are, and we know where you live."*

If you're still not convinced that this was a murder, ask yourself this question. When was the last time you were threatened for witnessing a car accident?

The reason for the demand of silence was to ensure that those who murdered Diana could lay the blame on the paparazzi. Witness testimony to the contrary was not going to be tolerated and if they opened their mouths further, they would have been silenced themselves.

This happened to one man who was a witness to the crash, but I'll save that story for later in the book. For the murderers the timing couldn't have been better. By the time the police arrived the assassins were long gone and all they saw were the Paparazzi, who had just arrived at the scene, and were snapping photos at close range of the Princess.

The police couldn't have been more disinterested in the eyewitness accounts as they rounded up the Paparazzi. In totality seven photographers: Romuald Rat, Jacques Langevin, Serge Arnal, Christian Martinez, Nikola Arsov, Laslo Veres, and Stephane Darmon were taken into custody where they were strip searched. Immediately, all of their film was destroyed, and their camera equipment was confiscated.

The authorities already knew that these seven people had nothing to do with the crash, but their real reason for holding, questioning and charging them was to learn what they actually knew, if anyone had tipped them off, and if so, who that might have been? More importantly they needed to destroy their film before it got out.

Photographic evidence of any kind is the last thing that hired assassins needed floating around. If photographs found their way into the tabloids, or worse, to an official investigation, it might contain undeniable evidence of a murder that would be impossible to ignore.

At this point another witness was ignored by authorities. Published in The Sun on August 21st, 2017 was an article written by Chloe Kerr. The article exposed the comments of a man named Stanlee Culbreath who was an attorney from Columbus, Ohio. Culbreath was in a taxi that was entering the tunnel immediately after the crash and was among the first people on the scene.

These are Mr. Culbreath's comments *"I was pleading with the officer to open the door... it looked like it could be pulled open. He wasn't doing sh*t. He wasn't doing anything." "She was always there for people in their hour of need, for the common man – but when her hour came, it seemed the response was sadly lacking."*

His eyewitness account was intentionally ignored by the French Police and by the British Inquest. This intentional lack of evidence and eyewitness testimony also explains why every traffic camera in the tunnel was either switched off or disabled at the time of the crash when they were usually live 24 hours a day.

To further ensure that no evidence existed, and the assassins wouldn't be caught, numerous break-ins would follow any path where photographic evidence might exist. The following excerpts are from Noel Botham's book entitled *The Murder of Princess Diana*. On pages 199 through 201 he writes...

"Twenty-four hours after the crash, two incidents took place at two separate addresses in London that bore a remarkable similarity to each other. At 3am, Lionel Cherruault, a London-based photojournalist, was woken at his home by his wife's screams. She had looked downstairs and seen that the front door was wide open. The police were called and Cherruault discovered, on checking his studio, that they had been robbed. His car had been moved and his wife's car stolen while they and their daughter had been asleep. The only thefts from the house were computer discs and electronic equipment used for storing and transmitting photographs. The discs contained a vast library of royal pictures and were the main targets."

"The previous morning, just after the crash in Paris, Cherruault had been offered photographs of the tunnel crash - but the deal collapses after Diana died. Even the police admitted it was no ordinary burglary. Cash, credit cards and jewelry were in full view when the computer equipment was stolen but had not been touched. Expensive cameras and lenses were also ignored. 'They had shut down the computers and actually removed all the hard drives,' said Lionel Cherruault.

'The next day, a man came to see me wearing a grey suit. He also had grey hair. He told me I had been targeted, not burgled, and hinted at government involvement. He said, "You can call them what you like - MI5, MI6, MI7, MI9, Special Branch or local henchmen - anything you like. But that person who came to your house had a key into you house and knew exactly where to go. But not to worry, your lives weren't in any danger."'

"Three hours earlier, and a few miles away in north London, Darryn Paul Lyons's photo laboratory was also broken into by mysterious raiders. By 3am on 31 August he had received crash photos, sent electronically from Paris by computer, from Laurent Sola, following a phone call shortly after 12.30am. High-resolution photos were received and Lyons, who runs Big Pictures photo agency, was negotiating deals with British and American outlets. The deals were called off after Sola telephoned with news of Diana's death."

104

"The following night between 11pm, 31 August and 12.30am, 1 September, the power to Lyons's office was mysteriously cut. 'When I returned to the office that night at 12.30am with colleagues I found I couldn't turn on any of the lights,' he said, in his statement to the police. 'It seemed as though we had suffered a power cut.

But other offices in the same building, and in other buildings nearby, remained alight, and the street lights were working. I heard an indistinct noise, like ticking, and thought a bomb was on the premises, so I told everyone to get out and called the police.' Lyons told police he believed secret-service agents had broken into his office and either searched the premises or planted surveillance and listening devices there."

Actions always speak louder than words and their actions were crystal clear. There was to be <u>NO</u> photographic evidence or witnesses to the crash, the tunnel, the flash of light or the assassins that caused it. In fact, the only photograph that was leaked to the public was a hand selected fake by the establishment to falsely show a mortally wounded Diana that would complement the story of her death.

The following circulated photograph erroneously shows the car without its roof and Diana in a position that was inconsistent with that of the authorities and the eyewitness statements. She also appears to be dead in the car, which she wasn't.

Decades later, after all the investigations and inquests were finished, the following black and white photograph was released. This is an actual photograph of Princess Diana taken immediately after the crash

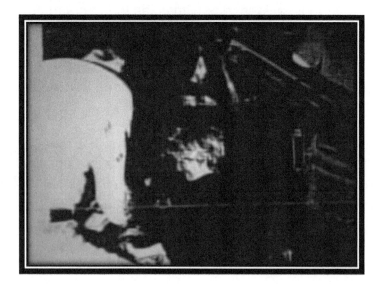

You can clearly see that Diana is very much alive, sitting upright, and grimacing in pain. Beyond question their governmental disinformation machine was running at full speed. Within 30 hours of arresting the paparazzi the French government realized that it would be impossible to hang Diana's death on photographers who were obviously not in the tunnel at the time of the crash and quickly changed their story to a new scapegoat.

The perfect scapegoat, the dead guy, Henri Paul. As suggested earlier in the chapter, those meeting at the Bilderberg Group needed an Oswald, and they found one, and like Lee Harvey Oswald, Henri Paul would be maligned as the guilty party for eternity.

Now, magically, before an autopsy or a toxicology report could have even been performed on Henri Paul's body, the story changed from the Paparazzi being the cause of the accident to a drunken driver who was driving erratically and lost control.

That concoction of lies became part of the official fiction and would prove to be a tidy story of the crash that was wrapped in a tight little package with a bow on it. Almost immediately, the French media, who were in full cooperation of the powers that be, plastered the story throughout Europe of Henri Paul causing the accident as he was 'drunk as a pig.'

The old saying is true, "dead men tell no tales." They also don't have alibis or hire defense attorneys. If they could, Henri Paul's name would immediately be cleared. After the crash police searched Henri Paul's apartment, not once, but twice. On the first search all the police found was a sealed bottle of champagne and a half bottle of martini.

This hardly supports the claim that Mr. Paul was an alcoholic and they quickly learned that pinning the crash on him was going to be a hard sell, so the media expanded their story to that of Henri mixing alcohol with anti-depressant drugs. This was also not true.

Searching for more clues they interviewed Claude Garrec, Henri Paul's best friend who insisted that Henri wasn't a heavy drinker and contrary to popular opinion, he wasn't a medication of any kind. Garrec's televised interview went as follows. *"Yes, focused [on the alcohol], they never mentioned he had 240 bottles of Coca-cola. Coca-Cola Light, which was his favourite drink. So why doesn't the report mention that? but when you stress the alcohol and ignore the soft drinks, well, that's distorted."* The interviewer asked Garrec *"Did they look for medication?"* Garrec *"Of course! No, they didn't find any medication, no."*

This televised interview gave the official fiction set by the state run media a very hard time, so the police returned to Henri Paul's apartment a few days later, and would you believe it, this time they found enough alcohol to stock three bars on Bourbon Street during Mardi Gras.

They claimed to have found beer, wine, bourbon, vodka, port, champagne and sherry. Afterall, it's easy to find alcohol when you're the one planting it there. Whenever anyone searches for something twice and finds what they are looking for in a gigantic quantity the second time, there's something very suspicious going on.

Try as they might to sell the story that Paul was "drunk as a pig" when the smoke cleared, the evidence revealed that Henri Paul was not drunk or under the influence, in any capacity, when he drove the Mercedes. According to witnesses, including Trevor Reese Jones, who has been with Paul for a time before he took the wheel, claimed that he was showing no signs of alcoholic impairment, if he had, Jones would have stopped him from driving immediately.

This fact was reinforced by an investigation launched by Dodi Al-Fayed's father who obtained Paul's bar bill which showed that the only alcohol he had that night were two Ricards (an anise and licorice-flavored Liqueur) that contains a mere 42% alcohol by volume. Henri had these drinks more than two hours before the crash. Drunk as a pig? Hardly.

Also illustrating that the previous facts were true were excerpts of the hotel's security video which showed Paul walking unimpaired and behaving quite naturally only moments before he drove. On the video he even bent down to tie both shoes without any complication or the slightest indication of losing his balance.

The world media's forced fed propaganda of Henri Paul was now losing all logical and scientific worth under the scope of investigation, and it's a good thing that Mohamed Al-Fayed's team investigated these claims, because neither the British or the French officials had in any dossier or investigation.

So, what actually happened that night to cause the fatal car crash? Diana had it right, partially. In a twist of fate that can either be deemed a conspiracy or a coincidence, Diana had left a note saying that somebody was going to kill her in a car accident.

It was her belief that this would happen due to the friction that was created between her ex-husband, Prince Charles, with the backing of his father, Prince Phillip, who held no affection for Diana in the latter part of their marriage.

She penned the premonition on her personal stationary from Kensington Palace in October of 1996 and gave it to her solicitor, Lord Mishcon. As the roses from her funeral were just beginning to wilt, Mishcon handed the letter to Britain's Chief Policeman, Lord Condon.

Condon reviewed the letter and did what any ethical law enforcement officer would do with a damning piece of evidence that could potentially solve a murder investigation - he concealed it - for three years.

He, in turn, gave the letter to his successor, Lord Stephens, who concealed it for another three years. For anyone keeping track, this evidence passed through the hands of three legally bound professionals who concealed it for a total six years.

These were puzzling feats for men, who by all accounts, were upstanding, stalwart and faithful officers of the law. So why would they break the very laws that they were sworn to uphold? To put this into painfully obvious terms, their actions make them a part of a criminal conspiracy by every definition in every country. The answer to my question was an obvious one.

If the letter had gone public, the whole world would have been talking about Diana's murder and they would have started pounding on a war drum for answers that would have held people accountable.

Based on the evidence that I have assembled throughout this exhaustive investigation, the crash, like the people who planned it, will be different from any of the promoted stories that the establishment has stuffed down your throat for the last several decades as they try very hard to convince you of something that is _not_ true.

This is what actually happened. The night of the crash, Dodi and Diana were chauffeured to Dodi's flat. Hours prior, Dodi had made dinner reservations. His plan was to have a quiet dinner with Diana, but when the time came for them to depart, at approximately 9:45pm, his security team advised him to abort the plans because there were several people loitering in front of the restaurant that looked suspicious; and they knew, what no one else did – Diana had been receiving death threats. Death threats that were not coming from the Royal Family.

The most public of these reports was published by The Sun on August 13th of 2017. The article that was penned by Sarah Ridley featured a man named Alan McGregor *"who worked for the Saudi Secret Service, was tasked with protecting the nation's royals at the Ritz in Paris in the months leading up to Diana's death on August 31, 1997."* The article continues *"he told how he once paid guerrillas £100million to stop them attacking Diana on her Red Cross trip to Angola."*

When I discovered this information, I began to investigate how many other times a ransom had been paid to protect Diana and more importantly, how many other threats she had received? I began my investigation into these questions by reaching out to The Sun hoping to contact Sarah Ridley. I did so by email and voice mail - 5 times.

I was ignored each time. I then tried to connect with Ms. Ridley via social media, but I was ignored there as well. Other stories that included Mr. McGregor's comments were picked up by The Mirror and the The Daily Mail. They also ignored my contact attempts. Why was no one talking?

My goal was to locate and interview Mr. McGregor, so I decided to sidestep these brick walls, and find Mr. McGregor directly. Unable to find him on social media, I reached out to a few of my contacts in military intelligence. I thought that surely, they could locate Mr. McGregor, but to my surprise, they were also unable to help me.

Now desperate, I contacted three Private Investigators in London who refused to acknowledge my email or return my call. If I do finally make contact with Mr. McGregor, I want him to share with me his ability to become invisible, because this is a disappearing act that is worthy of an Academy Award.

To return to the night in question; the couple decided, for security purposes, to stay at the Imperial Suit at the Ritz Hotel as the crowd that had gathered at the front entrance included well-known paparazzi but, much like the restaurant, several people began to loiter among them that looked suspicious and that no one could identify. The photograph below shows two of these men.

Photo courtesy of John Morgan

Henri Paul, now no longer needed as the couple was securely nestled in their luxurious hotel suit, left work and went to his apartment. There, he received a phone call from his MI6 contact telling him that the Ritz was no longer a safe place for the Princess and that the same people who were gathered earlier that night in front of the restaurant were now stalking the Ritz. This information was documented by at least three sources.

1.) The book *Death of a Princess: An Investigation* by Thomas Sancton and Scott MacLeod quotes the following *"Mohamed Al Fayed's lawyers submitted to Judge Stéphan thirteen photos, enlarged from Ritz security videos showing several unidentified individuals in the crowd. They have no cameras and are not dressed like tourists – they appear to be surveying the scene, their eyes looking intently in different directions. The photos have been included in the (French) dossier."*

2.) *A December 2004 article in The Daily Mail: "We know that…two (unidentified) men entered the Ritz and sat down at the main lobby bar. They ordered several rounds of drinks and remained, carefully observing events, until shortly before midnight…Their conversation was constant but very tense, In the article, the Mail calls the men "X and Y" for security reasons, but states that they are the two men named by Tomlinson i.e. Spearman and Langman according to the staff on duty."* The article continues *"Film footage (of the two men) is believed to have been seen by Scotland Yard, however the two men's faces are unclear and their identities have not been confirmed."*

3.) In a newsmagazine entitled Executive Intelligence Review. They claim that *"there were 7 unidentified men around the Ritz Hotel late on August 30 1997: 2 outside the Ritz apparently waiting and watching, 2 men in the bar of the Ritz, 2 men walking in and out of the Ritz, 1 man at the rear who made a mobile phone call as the Mercedes S280 departed."*

Incredibly, the Paget Report never addressed this evidence or investigated who the unidentified men were. Instead their focus was on an unidentified photographer claiming that he was loitering outside the Ritz nearly an hour before Diana's fatal crash. This is why Henri Paul's contact informed him that he needed to get the couple out of the Ritz and to take them to Dodi's flat, but in order to do so, he needed to use an alternative route that they had secured for the safe passage of the Princess.

The less traveled and less direct route that they had selected for him would ensure that they had open streets and that there would be no onlookers. They instructed him to use the cars at the front entrance of the hotel as decoys and to sneak the couple out of the back entrance. Luckily there was one car, and only one car remaining in the motor pool for them to use.

This way he could quickly get the Princess to their destination, and the crowd gathered in front of the Ritz would be none the wiser. With this information Henri Paul returned to the Ritz and explained what he had been told by his MI6 contact. Dodi, who was also concerned about the safety of the Princess, agreed and they began to put the plan into action.

This is the missing piece of the puzzle that has haunted Mohamed Al-Fayed every minute, of every day, since the crash. In the video *"Princess Diana: The Night She Died - Reel Truth History"* speaking in broken English he expresses his thoughts *"Dodi called me, it was about 12 o'clock. He say just I'm going now to the apartment, and he told me there were multiple paparazzi I don't know what to do the front door it's full of people."*

"I told him please, is so dangerous just stay in the hotel everything is there no need for you to go out. He told me, I think I will follow your advice. Why, after Dodi assured me that he's not gonna go out, uh, Henri pulled gun to him after 12 o'clock after Dodi talking to me and convince him no problem, we gonna go from the back entrance everything is okay don't worry, I know the way, and please you know because you have already prepared everything there, changed Dodi's mind."

Henri Paul knows that the car in the motor pool has clear windows, and that they are not at all tinted like the usual cars that are used by Dodi or his father. He surmises that one of his paparazzi friends could probably get some good photos through the windows and that he would be paid handsomely in return for his tip.

He notifies his paparazzi contact during the short period of time that he is missing from the security footage at the Ritz and then tells a bellboy to bring the car from the motor pool to the back door. Moments later Paul, Dodi, Jones, and the terrified Princess shut the doors to the Mercedes and begin their covert drive on their preplanned route. Within minutes two things happen that would change history. The Paparazzi, who were tipped off by Henri Paul, leave the front of the hotel and the passengers in the car that Paul is driving soon realize that they had been lied to. As the Mercedes leaves the Ritz it is quickly surrounded by a mysterious group of motorcycles that begin to box the car in and make threatening gestures toward the Princess.

As the Mercedes drove along Riverside Expressway in the first tunnel, the Alexandre III, the scene was described by witness Thierry Hackett *"[The Mercedes] was clearly being chased by several, I would say between four and six, motorcycles.There were two riders on some of the bikes. These motorcycles were sitting on the vehicle's tail and were trying to get alongside it." "I noticed that the Mercedes was veering from side to side....clearly, the driver of the vehicle was being hindered by the motorbikes."*

The passengers in the Mercedes are horrified by what's happening, and Paul presses the accelerator to the floor. In doing so he leaves his paparazzi friends far behind as the powerful engine of the Mercedes S280 began to hit spends that the photographers couldn't match; but the sinister motorcycles that are threatening the Princess have bigger engines and they continue to threaten the car.

Witness Brian Anderson gives his account *"The bikes were in a cluster, like a swarm around the Mercedes."* As the speeding Mercedes reaches the entrance to the Pont de l'Alma tunnel a small white car obstructs its path and intentionally clips its right side.

David Laurent, who was also driving in the tunnel, explains what he saw. *"I was surprised by a small car, which was driving at an abnormally low speed in the right lane. I do not understand why this car was going so slowly because nothing hampered its progression. It was an old model, light colored, white or beige, a Fiat Uno type car."*

Souad Moufakkir saw the white car and gives her account. *"I saw through the back window a Fiat Uno driving very fast up to us, in the outside [left] lane — but rather than hurtle past, it slowed down so we were side by side. It was very strange behaviour, and I got frightened. The white car was only centimeters from ours.... [The driver] had a very strange expression, like his mind was thinking about something else. His whole manner was odd. It troubled me.... I became very scared. I thought he was a madman, and I told Mohammed [the driver of her car] to speed away. We did that and later we heard the screech of tires."*

The final witness that has come forth with an account of what they saw in the tunnel was Francois Levistre and his comments are not only the most accurate, but they are the most compelling. *"I could see a vehicle surrounded by motorbikes. One of the motorbikes cut across the front of the Mercedes. There was a big white flash and then the car started to zigzag,*

*then it crashed. I thought it could be an assassination
or a gangland hit. I carried on driving as I did not want
any trouble."*

Levistre was spot on. Indeed, it was an
assassination attempt, and one that had been planned
out years in advance, but not for Diana. Sir Richard
Dearlove, former head of M16 admitted that his agency
had considered using the same formula in 1992 to
assassinate Serbian President Slobodan Milosevic.

Their plan was to force a crash as the target's car drove
into a tunnel by using a blinding flash device to
disorient the driver. This would force him to lose control
of vehicle. Months later, Dearlove's story was
confirmed by Richard Tomlinson.

Tomlinson was a decorated British Spy and MI6
officer beginning in 1991 until his firing from the agency
in 1995 when he announced he was authoring a book
about MI6 operations. As if firing Tomlinson, weren't
enough, in 1997 he served six months of a twelve
months prison on violations of the Official Secrets Act.

During his comments on this matter he verified
that *"Lights such as these are used as weapons by the
SAS in surprise raids. They blind and mentally
disorientate the enemy for up to a full minute."*
Tomlinson's comments on the subject are further
documented in the documentary entitled Unlawful
Killing.

"At first I just thought it was a joke and I refused to believe the officer when he told me about it. At first he outlined it to me verbally, and I went back to see him a couple of days later for another matter, and he sort of gave me a copy of that. He showed me the minute to sort of prove that he hadn't been joking about it. And so that's I remember that very clearly."

Curiously, in the murder of Princess Diana, several witnesses who were near the Alma Tunnel at the time of the crash reported seeing a bright flash seconds before the collision. When I discovered Tomlinson's comments, my mind immediately snapped to the conversation that took place at the Bilderberg Conference when one of the men said *"I know the people that can make that happen, and it's not their first time."*

I know this to be true as I have my own contacts within the industry and such high intensity operational strobe lights have even spawned the sale of personal use tactical flashlights that are now sold at the consumer level through television advertisements to stun and disorient a possible attacker.

In fact, that is one of the advertised selling features of these flashlights. Have you ever driven at night when some careless driver is coming at you with his high beams on? Imagine those flashes a hundred times brighter in a narrow tunnel. The results would be, well, exactly what they were.

If that wasn't enough of a coincidence, consider the mysterious death of Hollywood starlet Grace Kelly. In 1956, she abandoned Hollywood at the height of her career to marry Prince Ranier III of Monaco. In an eerie parallel to Princess Diana, millions of people watched her televised fairytale wedding on TV, her prince, like Diana's Prince Charles, was only faithful for a short time, and she would be killed, in a mysterious car accident, that would also be investigated by the French.

Her odd demise came in mid-September of 1982 as her Range Rover P6 3500 spun out of control on D37 highway in Monaco and plunged 120 feet off the side of a mountain. There were no skid marks on the road. Her daughter, who was with her in the car, claimed that she was screaming, "The brakes don't work. I can't stop" but that story didn't make sense upon investigation.

A September 6th 2018 Readers Digest article entitled "11 Unanswered Questions About Grace Kelly's Death" quotes the following *"British Leyland, the manufacturer of the Rover P6 3500, gave an official statement that this particular car had been fitted with a dual brake system that is literally "fail-safe."*

Captain Roger Bencze of the French police was put in charge of the investigation, and it also, like Diana's murder, involved members of the Royal Family who wouldn't let the investigator examine Kelly's body or interview her daughter.

In the end, the royal family was influencing another investigation of a dead princess and Captain Bencze was forced to blame the accident on two brain hemorrhages that the princess had in the hospital – after the crash.

In the planned murder of Diana, nothing that happened in tunnel that night was left to chance, not even the little white car whose glancing blow caused the Mercedes to crash into the concrete pillar.

The driver of the white Fiat Uno wasn't drunk, or driving erratically, he was planted there to perform a P.I.T. Maneuver on the Mercedes. A P.I.T. Maneuver which stands for "Precision Immobilization Technique Maneuver" is a tactical driving maneuver that was first invented and practiced in stock car racing in the early 1960's where a driver who was behind the target car would turn into their rear panel, causing the car to swerve from side to side to try and regain control. If they pushed the target car hard enough, and at a high rate of speed, it would turn sideways, spin out and abruptly crash.

Beginning in the early 2000's this and other avoidance maneuvers were taught to law enforcement officers in various countries to end high speed car chases. Prior to this, only professional drivers, stunt drivers or those who had been highly trained to use their car as a weapon were aware of this maneuver, and the driver of the white Fiat Uno was one of them.

Over the years wide speculation and investigation had been given to the identity of the Uno's driver ending in two possible drivers. One was a man named James Andanson. Andanson was a French photographer with long standing ties to MI6 as an informer who was eventually found in his Fiat Uno shot twice in the back of the head and then burned beyond recognition.

You don't need to be a conspiracy theorist to realize that the man was murdered. After all, it's awfully hard to shoot yourself twice in the back of the head and *then* set yourself on fire. Try that in any order you wish, I bet you can't do it. Go ahead, try it - I'll wait.

For those of you who are still with me, the other man that was identified as a possible driver was named Le Van Thanh. Van Thanh was located and questioned by the French Police, where he told them the truth, two different ways. First, he claimed that he was working as a security guard on the night of the murder, then the story changed.

Then he claimed that he was driving in Paris, but he was not in the vicinity of the tunnel. Again, you don't need to be a conspiracy theorist to realize that whenever you have two different answers to one question, you have a problem. He would eventually be questioned several times by authorities and authors who found him living in a palatial country home which was not a bad feat for a man on the salary of a security guard.

Many people have tried to interview Le Van Thanh without success. The most recent and well documented attempt was covered in the book *Diana: Case Solved: by Colin McLaren and Dylan Howard.* They write *"I headed out of Paris to a quiet little suburb with a number of houses tucked away in a back laneway. One house, a very big house, undergoing renovations, belonged to Le Van Thanh. A new Mercedes was parked on the driveway."*

"Le Vann and I shook hands. He then opened a pair of big steel gates that barred access to the property and the three of us stood on the driveway and I threw a few questions at the man—mostly as to whether he would allow me to tape-record the interview or film it. He kept smiling and shook his head; there would be no formal interview."

Either James Andanson or Le Van Thanh could have been planted to perform the P.I.T. Maneuver, but it really doesn't matter who did it, it was done with stunning accuracy. By this time the Mercedes was racing out of control, commandeered by the surrounding vehicles, it had received a glancing sideswipe from whoever was driving the white Fiat Uno, and it was heading 65 MPH directly for a concrete pillar that promised to be less than forgiving.

The only thing that remained to finish the job so the driver couldn't recover from the P.I.T. Maneuver was for the intense flash of light to be strobed into his eyes and the mission of the assassination team was complete.

I'd like to think that sometime before Henri Paul's car was surrounded by assassins and the time that his chest collapsed due to the steering wheel being catapulted through it, he realized that his MI6 informers who were working with the hired assassins had double-crossed him and used him as a sacrificial lamb.

From the minute that they set up the escape through the back door of the Ritz, they knew that he was going to be killed. This is a page right out of the mafias murder bible. If you're going to kill a target, always make sure you kill the informant as well. No one, NO ONE, can exist outside of the hit with information that could implicate anyone at a higher level.

This is something that Trevor Reese Jones, who I believe is a hero for trying to give protection to the couple in a situation that was impossible to achieve, understood in abundance. I believe Jones when he says that he can't remember anything about the crash, but I also believe it's that statement that has kept him alive.

After the horrific crash, in which the car stopped in the perfect P.I.T. Maneuver position, all of the assassins and their vehicles, sped out of the tunnel as planned and dispersed in different directions, never to be seen again. Right on their heels were the paparazzi who arrived at the crash scene moments later to find the crumpled luxury sedan with its horn blaring, steam hissing from the radiator, and smoke bellowing from what once was an engine compartment.

125

The tunnel was the perfect location for a designed crash. It's basically a tight concrete tube that allows for few witnesses. It has no safety walls or crash railings along the concrete pillars in the middle of the lanes and it can be turned into a deadly trap in the matter of seconds.

Henri Paul didn't even have time to hit the brakes. In fact, there were no tire marks to be found anywhere in the tunnel and the tire marks that were found on the road to the tunnel's entrance were examined by road-accident experts and were not caused by Diana's car. The assassination was flawless – almost.

When a traffic accident happens at 65 MPH, the car, your body and your internal organs all stop suddenly, creating a multitude of problems. That was the case for Diana. Although she wasn't instantly killed like Dodi and Henri Paul, and her gorgeous face wasn't ripped from her skull like Trevor Reese Jones, she was catapulted at 65 MPH into the back of Jones' seat causing internal damage.

As the paparazzi, witnesses, and other concerned citizens who heard the crash rushed to get help, or tried to aid the people inside the car, onlookers began to wonder where the ambulance was? I could never describe the situation as well as the narrator from the documentary "Unlawful Killing" has. In the movie the narrator explains.

"The crash occurred at 12:23 a.m. Dodi and Henri Paul died instantly. The Bodyguard Trevor Reese was seriously injured. Diana was injured but was conscious and alert, and had she received prompt hospital treatment she could well have survived, but she didn't. Instead an ambulance containing Dr. Jean-Marc Martino arrived at the scene."

"Although other ambulances were also present, he took sole charge of the princess and made a series of bizarre and disturbing decisions that sealed her fate. It took an astonishing 37 minutes after the crash for Dr. Martino to remove the still conscious Diana from the Mercedes and put her in his ambulance. Odd because the back of the car was undamaged.

It took an extraordinary 81 minutes after the crash before the ambulance even set off for the nearby hospital. Oddly it made no radio contact with ambulance HQ [at the hospital] throughout the journey. It took an inexplicable 1 hour and 43 minutes after the crash before the ambulance arrived at the nearby hospital, having traveled out at a snail's pace on empty roads."

" By then Diana's life was ebbing away. At the inquest experts agreed that her life could have been saved had it not been for the suspiciously slow and futile actions of Dr. Martino and his crew. The other members of which have never been officially identified or interviewed."

Diana was no ordinary woman. She was the most photographed and loved woman in the world and Dr. Martino had just taken her, with substantial internal injuries from a car accident, on the slowest ambulance ride in world history.

In contrast, Ronald Reagan, America's 40th President, suffered the same injury at 70 years old and survived because he received prompt medical treatment. Why was Diana not afforded the same opportunity of survival?

I believe there are two logical explanations. The doctor and his crew were either in on the assassination and wanted her "bleed out", or during the ambulance ride she was given an abortion, if indeed she was pregnant – which I doubt.

Rumors, as well as photographs, had widely been circulated claiming that the Princess was pregnant with Dodi's child, which couldn't be possible. The "Baby Bump" shown in the photograph on the next page is of a woman beyond ten weeks of pregnancy. Diana's relationship with Dodi lasted exactly four weeks which would make the fetus about the size of poppy seed.

It's medically impossible for Diana to be showing at four weeks of pregnancy. If there was a baby, it wasn't Dodi's. But let your mind ponder further, Diana's stomach is quite large in this bathing suit, but in photographs that followed, just days later, her stomach seemed to disappear.

This leads me to the logical explanation that the photograph was altered so it could be vended to the tabloids for a huge paycheck. I don't believe that there was any credence to the story of Diana's pregnancy, and I think it's time for everyone to move beyond this planned distraction.

That photograph, and the story surrounding it, was a plant to spin the story in another direction and cloud the investigation. I have also been told that Diana was using a body double during this time. Spend a few minutes examining the following photographs and ask yourself if this woman is *really* Princess Diana?

If this woman was a body double, and I said if, because no one knows for sure, it wouldn't be at all surprising. Many heads of state, as well as the ultra-famous among us, have used body doubles for years. Among them are Adolph Hitler, Howard Hughes, Elvis Presley, Vladimir Putin, Joseph Stalin, Andy Warhol, Winston Churchill, Queen Elizabeth II and Saddam

Hussein. Not to give into fantasy, but in Diana's case, with her getting numerous death threats, having a body double would make sense. Not only would it allow for added personal safety, it would also confuse any attempt for her assassins to properly track her. Are these body doubles? I'll let you be the judge.

Irrespective of your answer they still accomplished their goal of getting people to focus more on these photos, than on the facts of the murder. Promoted nonsense like this always clouds the real issue and spins people's attention away from the supreme importance of solving the case.

Aside from diverting the public's attention and confusing anyone who dares investigate these issues; people become personally and emotionally involved in defending their side of these supercilious debates, because no one enjoys being wrong. So, while the decades continue to roll by and fools endlessly debate both sides of this planted crap, the case goes unsolved and the murderers go free.

This is another classic example of thrusting supercilious nonsense into a murder investigation. The following photo of Lee Harvey Oswald has sparked endless debate for more than half a century on whether the shadowing was correct on the face versus the shadowing of the body.

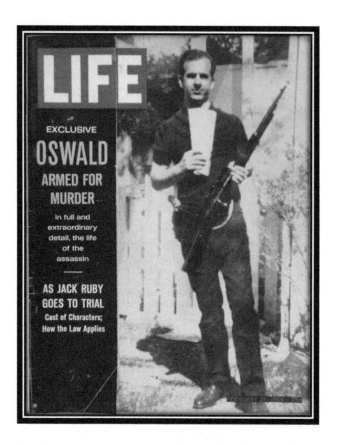

Pick your side and argue away, but none of these mental gymnastics matter as the photo served its real purpose of spinning people's attention away from investigating the real facts of the assassination. Once you know what to look for, this planted nonsense becomes easier, and easier to spot. For those of you who have read my book, *Who Murdered Elvis?*, a similar thing happened at Graceland. Someone planted empty drug syringes for investigators to find; without one needle mark on Presley's corpse.

Rewind to the assassination of President John Kennedy and the discovery of the legendary "Pristine Bullet" that was found on his hospital bed. This was another plant for the investigators to find for the sole purpose of causing confusion and fracturing the focus of their investigation. In case you haven't noticed, there's a pattern forming here.

Returning to the discussion the slow ambulance ride, the French have their own explanation, which is shaky at best. They claim that their SAMU ambulances are so well equipped that they can perform intricate procedures in transit and that their approach to emergency vehicles is different from other countries who use a fast ambulance to merely transport the victim to a hospital.

This made no sense to me at all, so I discussed it with one of my medical authorities, Dr. Cyril Wecht. Cyril has been an associate of mine since 2011 when we met through a mutual contact. Not only is he one of the best forensic pathologists in America having been President of both the American Academy of Forensic Sciences and the American College of Legal Medicine, he has also headed the board of trustees of the American Board of Legal Medicine.

Whenever I have a medial question or a question on an assassination, I can trust Cyril to give me a straight answer and this occasion was no different. Upon asking Cyril his opinion on the matter he replied, *"That's bullshit. The speed of the ambulance has nothing to do with what's going on in the back of it. The driver only has one job, to get to a hospital as fast as they possibly can. There's something very suspicious going on with that."* Diana's injuries from the crash were officially labelled as *"partial rupture of the left pulmonary vein at the point of contact with the left atrium."* When I asked Cyril if he thought that Diana could have been saved if she would have gotten medical attention sooner, he furthered his comments.

"If Diana could have been operated upon by a cardiovascular surgeon within 30 minutes, she might have survived. If IV fluids and other life support measures had been instituted within minutes she might have survived. For 45-60 minutes prior to surgery."

Dr. Wecht's expertise along with the testimony of several other medical professionals proves that the mysteriously slow actions of Martino and his crew contributed greatly to the death of the Princess. There was no good explanation as to why she was made to suffer in such a horrible capacity when three fully equipped ambulances were at the scene and two medical facilities existed only a few minutes away.

Even in death odd things continue to happen to Diana and Dodi as even their corpses broke the law. Dodi's body was flown back to Britain and buried the next day without an autopsy being performed in France.

This is against international laws. Dr. Wecht has informed me that due to many factors, including disease control, all bodies are to be autopsied in the country of their death. Dodi may have never broken the law, but his corpse certainly did.

134

What happened to Diana's body was equally strange. It was also flown back to Britain and when it landed it mysteriously became property of the Royal Family, who had it autopsied again.

This was odd as Diana was no longer a member of the Royal Family and several months earlier, they had insisted that she be stripped of her royal title. What right the Royal Family had to abscond Diana's body upon its landing was beyond any written law – but it happened.

Just when you might think that laws are taking a holiday when it comes to these two, apparently so did the calendar. British law states that inquests must be held when someone dies unexpectedly, violently or of unknown causes. The official wording of Britain's Coroners Act of 1988 states that *"the inquest should be held as soon as practicable."*

The official French inquiry into the deaths of Diana and Dodi Al-Fayed were held in 1999 and remains secret, but it apparently ruled out foul play. The British inquest of Princess Diana didn't begin until October 2nd 2007!

For any of you that are counting, the timespan between Diana's death of August 31st, 1997 and October 2nd, 2007 was 121 months. I don't know what your definition of *"as soon as practicable"* is, but I'm willing to bet that it's sooner than 10 years, 1 month and 3 days.

The inquest fiasco continued as the major news organizations prejudged it to be a waste of time and sent their royal reporters instead of their legal reporters. Legal reporters would have done their own digging would have challenged the proceedings, but royal reporters shamelessly suck up to their boss who are desperately seeking to be knighted by the queen.

Needless to say, no questions or probes would be launched and the whole inquest would play itself out for the joke that it was. Once the inquest began it was fairly obvious that substantial portions of the testimony were rehearsed well in advance and that the media bias wouldn't pose any obstruction to its flow.

It's impossible to cover the entire inquest within the confines of this book so what I'll do is concentrate on, what I believe, are the two biggest factors. The car and the alcohol content of Henri Paul. One must wonder why a Mercedes-Benz S280 would kill Dodi and Henri Paul in a collision in the first place.

Mercedes-Benz makes one of the finest and most well-constructed automobiles in the world that are crash tested at their facility for head on collisions at speeds higher than that which killed its passengers on impact.

In fact, the entire line of Mercedes-Benz automobiles have wonderful safety ratings. So why did this particular car fail? Mercedes-Benz was more than curious about the same question and offered to inspect the wrecked car for flaws and defects.

Partly because they wanted to protect their brand and partly because they thought that it was the proper thing to do. Either way you looked at it, from a public relations standpoint, they had everything to gain and nothing to lose by tendering their offer; an offer that was immediately and flatly denied.

That in itself was baffling. You would think that in any unbiased inquest this information would be useful, and you'd be right, but this was not an unbiased inquest. Instead of having the automaker inspect the vehicle, the inquest had the car examined by a crash expert on behalf of the Metropolitan Police.

Why have someone under the authority of the Metropolitan Police inspect the car instead of Mercedes-Benz? Because their crash expert was under the authority of the Royal Court, who was under the authority of the Royal Family, who was desperate to show the world that they didn't have a hand in Diana's murder, which they didn't, but damage control tactics still needed to be applied to their reputation.

The Metropolitan Police crash expert claimed that the vehicle was in perfect working order. That is, with the exception of Diana's seat belt. Diana always wore her seat belt, but on this night, it was impossible to do so because it was defective.

The Mercedes was being chased at high speeds which means that even if Diana didn't put her seat belt on when the trip started; she most certainly would have put it on as the dangerously high-speed chase intensified. Any one of us would have done the same.

This commonsense failure was more than hinting that the seat belt was jammed, and Diana, as well as Dodi, were prevented from using them. This is further evidence of pre-crash tampering with the Mercedes. Regarding the seat belt, I saved my final question for last, why was this information omitted from the inquest and conveniently not taken before the jury?

Let me state that again; the jury had no idea that Diana's seatbelt was jammed and that was a pretty important tidbit of information to conveniently overlook. Apparently, many other facts regarding the Mercedes were intentionally kept from the jury as well.

They were prevented from seeing the statement by the French Police claiming that the speedometer was stuck at 121 mph (196 kph), when Mercedes- Benz informed them that upon impact the speedometer of the car goes back to zero.

That statement by the French Police doesn't align at all with what the British are seeing so either the French and British authorities were lying about this detail – or they were looking at two different cars. The following quote is from page 418 of the Paget report.

"When examined by Police Capitaine Francis Bechet on 1 September 1997 the speedometer needle of the Mercedes car was at zero. When examined by Operation Paget following the transfer of the vehicle to the United Kingdom, the speedometer needle was in the 231 kph (144 mph) position. It was ascertained that

the speedometer needle could be moved manually to any position and that it would remain where placed. Operation Paget considers this movement to be normal."

The Paget Report continues to incorrectly comment on the overall safety and condition of the Mercedes according their Metropolitan Police crash expert. The fabled report continues. Page 424: *"On 25 May 1997 the vehicle steering geometry and wheel alignment were checked and minor adjustments made. This followed the theft of the (Mercedes S280) in April 1997, after which some repairs were carried out."*

"The French investigation reported the presence of stored data codes within some of (the electronic control) units. David Price (Paget expert) concluded that no additional testing was possible. He considered that the conclusions reached by the French investigators, that the codes had been created at the time of the crash, were most probably correct."

Page 425: *"David Price found nothing in his examinations of the mechanical elements of the car that would have adversely affected the control of the car or survivability of the occupants." "There were no defects on the vehicle that could have contributed to the causes of the crash."*

Report page 426: *"Both the French and British examinations of the Mercedes have shown that there were no mechanical issues with the car that could have in any way caused or contributed to the crash."*

The above comments fail to mention the following factors that could have affected the control of the car and the safety of the occupants:

1) A small penetrating cut in the side wall of the right front tire

2) Several missing fuses

3) Presence of moisture in the brake fluid

4) Stored data codes in the car's computer showing issues with the electronic control units

Possibly of greatest concern in the above list are the missing fuses and the codes that were stored in the car's computer. A car's computer codes tell many things when they are read, and the information is broken down. So, at this point, a clear minded person would certainly ask the Mercedes-Benz corporation for an analysis, or at the very least, one would dig into the owner's manual examining the information for inclusion into the report. Neither were done.

Were they trying to find evidence of possible electronic tampering, or trying to hide it? Hold this question in your mind as we dig into the mysterious background of this vehicle. The following information was cited by many sources but none better than *Hounan & McAdam* in their book *Who Killed Diana*. They write *"Earlier that year the car, which was kept at the Ritz for the exclusive use of its guests, was stolen in mysterious circumstances."*

*"On duty for the hotel, the car was parked outside the
exclusive Taillevent restaurant on the rue Lamennais
waiting for guests to finish their meal. Without warning,
the driver's door was flung open and the chauffeur
dragged from the vehicle by three Arabic-speaking men
wielding handguns."*

*'It was like a commando attack,' the driver said later.
The vehicle disappeared for nearly two weeks before
turning up in Montreuil in a distressed condition. The
wheels were gone, the door had been ripped off, the
complete electronic system and the box controlling the
ABS braking system had been stolen.*

*The Mercedes France dealer in Saint-Quen where the
vehicle went for repairs costing 15,000 Francs ($2,750)
reported it was the work of professionals."* Further
investigation into the matter came across Christopher
Andersen's work entitled *The Day Diana Died: "The
(Mercedes S280)...had been parked in front of
the...Taillevent Restaurant on April 20 (1997) when it
was stolen, then stripped for parts and abandoned
outside Paris."*

*"Recovered sixteen days later, the car was missing,
among other things, the wheels and tyres, the inner
workings of the doors, and the electronic 'brain' that
controls key functions – from the power steering and
power windows to the speedometer, the anti-lock
braking system, and the...engine itself. Total cost of
repairs $US20,000."*

This evidence shows a clear, concise and intentional collusion between the French and British governments to hide the actual facts of the condition, faulty repair work and possible tampering with the Mercedes S280 that carried Princess Diana and two other passengers to their death.

Incredibly, I am not alone in my assessment of these facts as the elusive Alan McGregor, who was responsible for protecting the Royal Family at the Ritz Hotel, claimed that a detailed plot to kill Diana could have been planned several months prior.

I discovered this as well as the following quotes in an article dated August 13th 2017 by The Sun. McGregor's comment tells me that the tip that I received about the Bilderberg Group meeting was spot on, as the timeline aligned perfectly.

In reference to the selection of the car and the lack of security at the rear entrance McGregor continues: *"it was the biggest security breach he knew of in six years of working at The Ritz." "They also got that car from the hotel's public car park rather than the secure underground one." "Why was it driven by a bellboy? It should have been a specially-trained driver or a security agent. He could have been anyone."*

These were also great points that were not raised by the French or the British governments during their investigations. Why? The answer to that question is a simple one, because these facts didn't suit their narrative or the lies that they were selling.

The evidence is conclusive. The same car that carried the Princess to her untimely demise had been stolen, stripped, partially repaired, and was parked in an unsecured lot where anyone could have tampered with it. Compounding these unsettling facts was the mysterious bellboy previously mentioned by Alan McGregor.

Who was he? Was he in on the plot? Could he have jammed Diana's seat belt? It's quite possible that the hired assassins who told Henri Paul to return to work and take Dodi and Diana out the back entrance had all of this arranged as they sent their informant, Henri Paul, off to slaughter.

In the grand scheme of things Paul was expendable and in their eyes his death was a minor detail standing in the way of the huge sum that they received for murdering Diana. McGregor's comments in that article continue to mirror mine in the following series of quotes about his fellow co-worker and security agent, Henri Paul.

"Paul wasn't a drinker at all. I never saw him buying alcohol. He just wasn't that sort of bloke. It doesn't make any sense." "I'd been through that tunnel so many times too and it would have been almost impossible to hit that pillar." "And Henri Paul had been appointed their driver but he wasn't qualified either." "There was no way he should have been put in that position."

McGregor's comments about Henri Paul, his alcohol habits, or, rather, the lack of them, leads me to the second point that I will question in the inquest. Henri Paul's blood alcohol content at the time of the crash and the lies surrounding it.

The first mysterious thing that happened after this horrific crash (aside from the world's slowest ambulance ride) was that the car was immediately loaded on a flatbed and hauled through the streets of Paris at 2am destroying key evidence. This was beyond tolerance.

You only get one chance to investigate a crime scene. Once a crime scene is touched or altered in any way, all hopes of a thorough investigation are lost. That's why police investigators put up yellow tape around the perimeter of a crime scene – to keep everyone out of it. Otherwise, crime scene tape wouldn't exist.

By not preserving the death scene, any competent investigation would not have been impossible. Were the people looking at the wrecked Mercedes removing evidence or planting phony evidence to deflect the investigation? Who knows because nothing was preserved and crime scene investigators were never called.

After the car was removed, the unthinkable happened. Shortly after Diana was pronounced dead, French Police called in a road sweeping van to wash away whatever debris, evidence or other fragments that remained on the road, on the pillar, or on the opposite wall of the tunnel. Whether this was a traffic accident or not, something of this magnitude involving the Princess of Wales should have told them that the tunnel needed to be shut down and the scene preserved.

No logical person on this planet who wanted to investigate a suspicious crash would do this but, incredibly, it happened. This is very similar to the Pakistani police washing away the evidence where Benazir Bhutto, Prime Minister of Pakistan, was assassinated.

After those two inexplicable acts happened, the third happened: thirty hours after the crash. newspapers in France began running a story that Henri Paul was drunk and in a matter of two hours he was found guilty before the world in their court of public opinion.

That was the story that the state-run media had concocted and that was the story that they were sticking to. Unfortunately, it wasn't possible. John MacNamara, former Director of Harrods' Security who led the private investigation into the death of Diana for Mohamed Al-Fayed commented on this very issue.

"Within just over 24 hours of this crash, when it was put out that this was caused by a drunk driver. A person drunk as a pig driving at 192 kilometers [119.30 MPH]. They were false statements. They were certainly false statements then, and we know they're false statements now. And one of the reasons

we know that is that the statement as to the drink drive was put out <u>before Henri Paul's body had even been analyzed</u>. So they didn't have an analysis report of this and yet it was put out that he was drunk. Severely drunk."

Where did this lie come from? The French authorities. The same people who ruined the evidence of the crash scene so there could be no investigation. They leaked the information to the press that Diana's driver was severely drunk which was a baseless claim.

This is a parallel situation to the probe (or rather the lack of it) into the mysterious death of Elvis Presley and the press conference given by the Medical Examiner, Jerry T. Francisco, the same Medical Examiner who also botched MLK's autopsy a few years prior.

Before the Presley autopsy was even halfway completed, before the toxicology reports had been received and without one fingerprint being lifted at Graceland; Francisco told the press that Elvis died of cardiac arrythmia within a few hours of receiving his body.

This is incredible when you consider that in the case of Marilyn Monroe's postmortem examination it took Dr. Thomas Noguchi 11 days to go public with his findings. For Elvis to be diagnosed with cardiac arrythmia his heart would have needed to have been examined while it was beating - but it wasn't.

Meanwhile more parallels between Elvis' murder and Diana's murder appear as his death scene was mysteriously sanitized and, like the burglary of Diana's photos after her death, the investigator for the Presley murder had his notes and photos of the death scene stolen from his car seven hours after the investigation.

Like the Paget Report, Francisco's diagnosis of cardiac arrythmia (irregular heartbeat) was widely accepted and published by the press leaving Vernon Presley, Elvis' father, who knew that he was murdered, to hire two private investigators to try and solve the crime. To complete this eerie parallel, Mohamad Al-Fayed did the same thing in his search for the truth which poked holes in the official fiction of the Paget Report.

In my second book, *Who Murdered FDR?*, President Roosevelt's widow, and former first lady, Eleanor, hired a private investigator in 1957, twelve years after FDR's death, in an attempt to quiet the rumors of his murder.

In the end, all she would discover was that FDR's medical records had been stolen from a locked filing cabinet at Bethesda Naval Hospital, the same place where JFK's autopsy would be botched, and his brain would vanish.

The parallels among the Who *Murdered Elvis?, Who Murdered FDR?,* and *Who Murdered Diana?* books cannot be dismissed. The autopsy of Henri Paul, which included the toxicology report, was performed by Toxicologist Dr Gilbert Pepin and Forensic Pathologist Dominique Lecomte. Lecomte, who was notorious for hiding medical evidence that was likely to embarrass her superiors or the French authorities who fudged the autopsy results.

The documentary *Unlawful Killing* quotes the following: *"If her own account is to be believed, she conducted the world's worst autopsy on the corpse of Henri Paul committing at least 58 basic errors. Every medical expert at the [British] inquest agreed that her results were not only inept, but biologically inexplicable too – and that her report was untruthful."*

What further indicated that the blood sample that was analyzed was not that of Henri Paul were extreme levels of carbon monoxide. The carbon monoxide level in Paul's blood was so high that he would have not been able to walk, which he did quite well on the video produced at The Ritz hotel by those investigating the crash.

Further, if Paul really was an alcoholic this would have been diagnosed during the stringent medical examination that he underwent three days before the crash to renew his pilot's license, but he passed the medical examination without incident.

Upon learning of these new facts Lord Justice Scott Baker, who sat as coroner for the Royal inquest, requested the appearance of Forensic Pathologist Dominque Lecomte and Toxicologist Dr Gilbert Pepin to investigate and question their findings.

They refused to appear; and although they were legally bound to as they were citizens of the European Union, the French government stated that they needed to be protected due to "protection of states secrets and the essential interests of the nation." In short, that meant the French government and their officials were covering their asses.

Oddly, neither the British inquest, or the French investigation interviewed or questioned the doctor who gave Henri Paul a clean bill of health for his pilot's license, which to me is another staggering failure on the behalf of the investigators. I guess the old saying is true, only look for what you want to find.

At this point it has become fairly obvious that the blood sample tested could not have been from the body of Henri Paul, and three questions must be asked. Whose blood sample was it? How did it get switched? Was it intentional?

Six other bodies were in the morgue on the night when Paul's blood sample was taken, and all of the samples had been extracted for the purposes of toxicology reports. The clear plastic vials were filled with blood and placed in a holder, where, one by one, the necessary tests were carried out.

Then the vials were labeled and stored; but there was a problem with this procedure. The person who extracted the blood was not the same person who ran the testing and labeled the vials, which may explain why Henri Paul's name is misspelled on his sample.

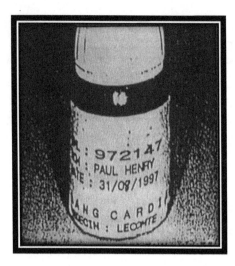

Photo courtesy of John Morgan

The blood sample isn't even out of the laboratory yet and already a glaring mistake has been made. Beyond question the procedure of extracting and testing the blood samples were rife with errors, errors that were far beyond misspelling the man's name on the label. This was intentional.

The blood needed to be tainted for Paul to be their scapegoat. After the paparazzi were released from blame, they needed to give the naive public a villain to make them go away and stop probing further. Their toxicology report was a jumbled farce.

The authorities at the inquest agreed with me as they signed a joint statement declaring that the blood test results for Henri Paul were "biologically inexplicable." Further proof that the French and British authorities knew of this error was covered in the documentary unlawful Killing.

150

"Why did Britain's top policeman, Lord Stevens, tell Henri Paul's parents in 2006, in front of other policemen who kept a written record of the conversation, that their son was definitely not drunk, he asserted and that Henri was not drunk on the evening of the accident and that he was driving at a lower speed than what was indicated in the French proceedings. Yet six weeks later Lord Stevens published a report claiming that Henri Paul was drunk, so who was lying? Lord Stevens or Lord Stevens?"

My number one question when I learned that neither country involved in the testing of the blood sample could manage to handle it in a professional manner was to ask if anyone had bothered testing the DNA of the sample to see if it actually matched Henri Paul.

You would think that if an investigative author living halfway around the world (speaking of myself) could ask such a question, that trained professionals, who have done this work for years, could have figured this out on their own.

We can add this to the laundry list of things that people involved in this case forgot to do correctly, even though this is the job that they do every day – year, after year, after nauseating year. Now either these people were paid to do their jobs wrong, or this oversight was intentional. Naturally, that's a hypothetical question because we already know the answer.

Finally, nine years after the crash, autopsy and erroneous toxicology report; a team of scientists had an epiphany and offered to carry out a DNA analysis on the blood samples to determine if the sample that everyone had been discussing since 1997, was actually the blood of Henri Paul.

When they inquired, they were told by the French authorities that samples had been discarded, which I'm sure they had been, as fast as humanly possible. This seems to fit the narrative as no one preserved the crash scene, the tunnel, and no one was allowed to inspect the car except someone who was paid not to find anything. Does this make sense to you? No? That makes you smarter than the "professionals" involved in the investigation. Mother Goose couldn't write a nursery rhyme like this.

Amazingly this is where the team of scientists stopped their search, but there had to be blood from Henri Paul on the driver's side of the car that could have been analyzed. In fact, if you look closely in the photos of the crash, you can see his blood.

So, from here I have to ask a further question. Is this where the scientists stopped on their own; or is this where the scientists were stopped by others? Why would they stop so quickly at a chance to go directly to the blood source and end decades of speculation? It's a question that is certainly worth asking but one else has.

To add another wrinkle to the investigation that has been overlooked for decades; what about the investigation of the concrete pillar? Concrete has very specific properties when cured and the impact mark left on the pillar would have certainly given a clue as to the speed and angle of the car on impact.

You don't need to be Sir Isaac Newton or Albert Einstein to calculate a simple acceleration times mass formula and test it against the cured mixture of the concrete that was used in the pillar. How about running these tests on the pillar next to it?

Obviously, the pillar next in line was poured at the same time, was the same age and had the same mixture of aggregate. I have no doubt that the hydration process in the next pillar would be the same.

Further, where were the laser pointers or other devices that could have been used to determine the angle of impact? The properties of concrete are something that I am well acquainted with as I have a Construction Degree (as well as others) and I have been tested at length on its attributes.

I would gladly undertake such an investigation, but something tells me that if I were asked, the night before I arrived, the thirteenth pillar would be altered in some way making conclusions that should have happened decades ago impossible.

More oddities were found in the behavior of the media. Why weren't the British press corps more suspicious of these findings and start searching for answers on their own? Don't they have investigative journalists in Britain? Instead, they took an almost zen-like approach to the entire inquest acting as disinterested as they possibly could.

How about the country of France? Don't they have investigative journalists in France? These are a few of those "macro questions" that I mentioned in chapter 3 that answer most of the "micro questions."

I guess it's hard to investigate something when your current position depends on you not investigating it. Diana was correct about predicting her fatal accident, but she was incorrect as to whose hands the accident would be orchestrated by.

It wasn't the crown, although they weren't thrilled with her constant barbs, it was a group of hired contractors using their intel who were hired by the Armament community to do the assassination and make it look like an accident.

Once their target had been killed, the French police had no answers and went into damage control mode. They needed to do three things immediately and in sequence, and with great precision. They needed to twist the facts with media spun propaganda, they needed to find someone – anyone - to blame, and lastly, they needed to manufacture evidence to sell the story.

Each were done with incredible success. This answers another "macro question" which more than explains why the standard procedures of bodyguards, motor pools, cars, drivers, law enforcement officers, ambulances, autopsies, and inquests seem not to apply to these two people - in any country.

So, at this point I must honestly ask, is this a conspiracy theory or a conspiracy reality? The purpose of the inquest was to investigate the suspicious circumstances surrounding the crash, but their investigation ignored any/and all parts of the coverup that the French hadn't already lost, dismissed, or omitted. Clear eyed people should have seen that this was not exactly the place where an impartial court was going to judge anything, but it would eventually spawn the oddest of coincidences.

Stephens and Condon broke the law by withholding Diana's handwritten letter that she gave to her attorney predicting that she would be killed in a car crash. Both men broke the law and both men were made lords by the queen for protecting their image; an image that was surely to be tarnished beyond repair if indeed it appeared that the crown were involved.

Desperate people do desperate things, and the Royal Family was desperate for damage control because the possibility that they would lose the Monarchy was very real. In the end, the jury of the Inquest determined that Diana and Dodi were victims of an "Unlawful Killing" but to this day, decades later, no one has been arrested for these killings and no action has been taken by any agency to hunt down those responsible or bring them to justice. In fact, all of the paparazzi vehicles have been identified and excluded from the investigation, but none of the drivers of the motorcycles that actually caused the crash have been. So again, I have to ask another "macro question" - why haven't the French or British police been tracking down the killers?

The answer is a chilling one. They already knew who they were, and this isn't the first time that they have all worked in concert with them. In any country in this world that isn't a theory, that's a conspiracy.

The timeframe of Diana's death wasn't picked by chance, it was carefully calculated and needed to happen before September. In June of 1997 the second meeting of the ICBL (International Campaign To Ban Landmines) met in Ottawa where 100 countries endorsed a declaration affirming their intention to sign a treaty creating a total ban on anti-personnel landmine use before the end of the year.

The next meeting to accomplish this was scheduled for September 19th, and it was a conference that the Princess wasn't meant to attend. Less than three weeks after the crash, with Diana dead, the world's press didn't even bother to attend the conference to see US President Bill Clinton become the only western leader to vote against the ban.

An odd reversal for the American President who, on May 16th said *"to end this carnage, the United States will seek a worldwide agreement as soon as possible to end the use of all anti-personnel landmines."* What changed in four months? Was this the real reason that the American Secret Service had almost 1200 pages of transcription of Diana's phone conversations?

Further proof that this was a blatant assassination can be found in the threatening and/or assaulting of witness Eric Petel, witness Trevor Reese Jones, investigator John Morgan, the continued harassment of the Firestone family, and the firing / jailing of former MI6 Agent, Richard Tomlinson (among others). Again, I have to ask a very logical question. Have you ever been threatened or harassed for witnessing a car accident?

Diana's anti-landmine campaign was upsetting the world's armament industry and threatening to bankrupt the economies of smaller countries in the process. At the same time her relationship with Dodi, Mohammad Al-Fayed's son, and longtime thorn in the side of the British royalty, was making the Monarchy's blood boil.

Princess Diana already had the rare ability to go above the ambitions of world governments and captivate the population for her causes, which anguished the globalists and their intentions.

These globalist leaders became apoplectic with rage at the thought of her influence and weapons bans combined with a billionaire's bankroll to promote it. Diana was unknowingly, and naively, hijacking the world's agenda away from some very, very big players.

She simply couldn't pull this off and live and they took a page right out of the mafia's murder book to "make it look like an accident." You might think that the gathering of all of this information and the obvious conspiracy surrounding it to murder Diana had never happened on a scale this large before, but you'd be wrong.

6
The Requiem

The murders of Diana, Elvis, FDR and JFK all have commonalities that are impossible to ignore. Botched autopsies, missing or stolen documents, faulty investigations, the departure from standard practices and procedures, deaths that were immediately blamed on dead assassins by the controlled media and quickly sanitized death scenes - just to name a few.

Are we really expected to believe that these anomalies were mere coincidences and that hundreds of highly trained professionals suddenly forgot how to do their jobs? Obviously, these murders were all written out of the same script as the odds of these circumstances occurring without a connection would be like winning the lottery in every country around the world on the same day.

Coming to that realization was a bitter pill for me to swallow because I am far less of conspiracy seeker and far more of a history detective; but historical facts never lie. The fingerprints of conspiracy are all over the deaths of these people and for some reason no one, outside of myself, wants to investigate them.

Most likely because they are afraid to be labeled a conspiracy theorist which would insinuate that they are suffering from some variety of delusion or insanity.

According to The Cornell Law Library, this is the legal definition of conspiracy: *"An agreement between two or more people to commit an illegal act, along with an intent to achieve the agreement's goal."* The term "Conspiracy" has nothing to do with wild-eyed theories or insane conjecture as the over used term "Conspiracy Theory" suggests.

It amazes me how this legal term has morphed. Today the widely repeated term "Conspiracy Theory", which was born out of the aftermath of the Kennedy assassination to label anyone who questioned the findings of the Warren Commission Report as a nut, has evolved. It's now attached to anything that people don't understand, like or agree with.

Possibly that was the CIA's intention from the beginning. In court, those trying to prove that a person is guilty would love to label everything that they don't want you to investigate as a "Conspiracy Theory" to shame everyone away from going down roads that might contain actual evidence.

It's irrational, illogical and irresponsible to label all conspiracies as "theories" as there are real people, in court, right now, for conspiracy who certainly wish that they weren't.

So, tell me who the crazy people are? Are the "Conspiracy Theorists" who attempt to find actual information to solve events the crazy people, or are the narrow-minded simpletons who blindly repeat only what they've been told the crazy people? Think about your answer very carefully because smart people always seem crazy to dumb people.

If I'm walking outside and my head starts getting wet and I look up to see if it's raining - am I a "Conspiracy Theorist"? Where does the line get drawn? Frankly, I think we need to make a name for the stupidest among us who are incapable or unwilling to think on their own and generate individual thoughts.

Maybe it's time to flip the script because my bullshit filter is full, and I can't take much more of the narrowminded thinking that exists, seemingly without boundaries or limits, and is being spewed from the mainstream propaganda channels on an hourly basis.

If you want to call me a "Conspiracy Theorist", a label that I detest, as it infers someone presenting a theory without evidence, I'll survive. I'm from a different generation that wasn't haunted by the peer pressure of political correctness (also known as, think my way or be punished).

I'm not a frail shrinking flower who needs to belong or be accepted and I won't tremble and pee my pants when I'm cross examined. My facts of conspiracy speak louder than any voice on the network news and I'm happy to share them with you.

On the grander scope of things, there's nothing unique about the assassination of Princess Diana. Earlier in the book we've already covered the assassination and coverup of Benazir Bhutto, Prime Minister of Pakistan, and Princess Grace of Monaco.

Diana's assassination is just another example where the target of the hit and the cover up followed the same pattern. When you've investigated as many of these assassinations as I have you begin to see common threads. I like to call these "threads of insanity" because you'd have to be insane not to see the commonalities in their murders.

In simple terms, whenever you start seeing phony evidence added to a death scene that shouldn't be there, or evidence removed from a death scene that should be there, that's a telltale sign that you're dealing with a professional hit and you'll never find the answers that you're looking for.

Cover ups are always more conspiratorial than the actual murder because they require more people to act in concert to twist, hide and contort the pieces of evidence so they can't be traced back. It's also harder to keep everyone on the same page which is why making everything look like an accident is ideal, especially if there's a car involved.

An automobile is the ultimate murder weapon because fatal car accidents are very common, and they are much easier to "explain away" to the average person who wouldn't know actual evidence if they tripped over it. The more you're able to "explain away", the less involved everyone has to work to cover it up.

In the last chapter, when I debunked the altered photo that was planted as evidence claiming that Diana was pregnant, I mentioned similarities between the photo and the bogus drug syringes planted at the Elvis Presley death scene, and the legendary "Pristine Bullet" that was planted on JFK's hospital bed.

These were all meant to be found to confuse the investigation by entering phony evidence. Now I'd like to add a few more of these planted items to the mix. Former Heavy Weight Champion Sony Listen was found dead shortly after he refused to intentionally lose a fight against Chuck Wepner. When his corpse was found, days later, there was drug paraphernalia on the kitchen counter and in his pockets. There were also needle marks in his arms, but he wasn't a drug user.

He hated drugs and a would often lecture young people about how dangerous they were. Further, he was so afraid of needles that his dentist testified that he would faint at the sight of them and needed to be put to sleep to have his dental work done. Odd to find needle marks in his arm, especially when the autopsy showed no drugs in his system. The description of his corpse also matched Elvis Presley's to a tee. Nude from the waist down and frothing from the mouth.

Marilyn Monroe, another one of my distant cousins, was also victim to the "threads of insanity" as her death scene not only had planted evidence to confuse the police, it was sanitized, and staged. When police arrived, they immediately noticed that someone had staged a burglary by breaking the glass leading to her bedroom, but the broken glass fragments were on the outside of the bedroom, not on the inside. No one breaks out of a house, especially when the broken window is right next to a door.

They also discovered that Monroe's body was found lying on the wrong side. The purplish tint that occurs on the surface of the skin when a person dies, is caused by the blood pooling when the heart stops beating. This gravitational pooling of blood is called Livor Mortis and it always pools at the lowest levels of the body.

In the case of Marilyn Monroe, Livor Mortis was on the wrong side of her face. When investigators examined her body more closely, they saw that her face had the purple side up – not down. The immutable laws of science don't change because the dead body is famous, and they immediately knew that there was an issue.

Her body, as well as the entire death scene, was loaded with planted evidence and red flags. Sgt. Clemmons of the LAPD was the first to arrive and publicly stated that the scene *"looked like it was staged."* He did not, however, answer the question that everyone was asking. Why was it staged to look that way?

164

There are literally dozens of examples of high-profile people who have either crossed the wrong people or their management was involved in dirty dealings that have suffered a similar fate at the hands of hired assassins.

The photo of Diana's pregnancy perfectly mirrored the drug syringes planted by the murderer at Elvis Presley's death scene, the drug paraphilia planted at Sony Listen's death scene, the broken window at Marilyn Monroe's death scene, as well as the pristine bullet that was planted on JFK's hospital bed.

All of these carefully planted artifacts were placed to confuse the investigation and to spin the heads of anyone who tried to put the pieces together. This is what these people do for a living, folks, and they're good at it.

The death scenes of Marilyn Monroe, Princess Diana, Elvis Presley, and JFK were immediately sanitized to remove evidence that might have been discovered by a criminal investigator, so they had nothing to work with.

Marilyn Monroe's maid was doing laundry from her death scene when the police arrived, the tunnel where Diana's murder happened was immediately cleaned, and EMT's at Elvis Presley's death scene reported signs of a struggle to investigators but when they returned to Graceland everything, including the carpet, had been cleaned.

In the case of JFK, the President had just been carried into Parkland Memorial Hospital with a very serious gunshot wound to his head, and Secret Service Agents were seen wiping the blood splatter off the interior of the Presidential Limousine with buckets of water and sponges.

JFK's Secret Service Agents were actually being told to alter a crime scene before any investigation could be conducted - and then - JFK's brain disappeared. Yes, you read that correctly, his brain. How the hell do you lose the brain of a slain US President hours after he was shot in the head?! These aren't conspiracy theories; these are conspiracy facts. These things happened.

Presley's stomach contents, that were mysteriously rinsed down a drain before the autopsy, could have revealed many things about his final hours in the same way that JFK's brain could have revealed the type of bullet, the type of gun and the trajectory of the shots. My friend, Dan Warlick, was the investigator for the Medical Examiner in the Presley case, and spoke to me on many occasions about the mysterious Graceland cleanup.

Someone even made Elvis' bed before the investigators arrived, but no one admitted to it. To read the entire eye popping account, pick up a copy of *Who Murdered Elvis?*. It's the perfect read for anyone who has been fooled into believing that Elvis died from a heart attack, a drug overdose or is somewhere roaming the earth.

166

There are also parallels between the murders of FDR and JFK. Both President's met their demise away from Washington D.C. FDR was murdered in the state of Georgia and JFK was murdered in the state of Texas. Both bodies were immediately removed from those states and brought back to Bethesda Maryland without being autopsied in the states in which they died.

This is in violation of both state and federal laws, but both administrations did it. FDR's secret service did it in 1945 and JFK's secret service did it in 1963. As you can see, the more famous you are when you get murdered, the more laws your corpse seems to break.

To fully understand the gravity of the laws that were broken and how infiltrated Roosevelt's administration was, pick up a copy of *Who Murdered FDR?* as I can't do justice to this subject in the space allotted.

I have no doubt that someone in the mentally challenged mainstream media would lead you to believe that these things didn't happen, but they did – all of them. It just takes someone, like me, who has studied and published books on these murders for 15 years to be able to string all of these extraordinary coincidences together.

As I said in chapter three, there are both micro and macro questions in every murder investigation that need to be examined, but it takes someone with a unique mindset to examine them and realize that looking at one of these murders by itself is like looking at one blade of grass in a lawn.

Now you can understand why the hairs on the back of my neck stood up when I saw the "Threads of Insanity" so clearly in Diana's case and how clearly it mirrored the investigation into President Kennedy's assassination. When I saw the obvious errors in the Paget Report it struck me as a carbon copy of the 888-page Warren Commission Report which was rammed down the public's throat on September 27, 1964.

The inquest, investigation and the findings were so exact that it almost looks like the Warren Commission Report was used as the template for the lies and misdeeds that were illustrated in the Paget Report.

Aside from the obvious takeaways from these two assassinations, that both victims were killed in their cars as they were being chauffeured to their intended destinations, and both targets were contract killings with government involvement, are the parallels of their abnormally slow delivery to the hospital.

Diana had the slowest ambulance ride in world history and JFK's driver, when the shots rang out, stopped the car. This can be clearly seen in photographs as the taillight on Kennedy's limousine was lit. Odd, when both situations called for immediate speed to potentially save their passengers lives.

To continue to brush the very surface of the similarities between these two assassinations were the identities of the drivers themselves. Henri Paul wasn't Diana's usual driver nor was he officially trained or licensed to act as a chauffeur.

In the case of JFK, William Greer, the chauffeur who drove Kennedy to his death, wasn't his usual driver either and as the decades have passed, both Paul and Greer have come under intense scrutiny for their potential roles in the assassinations.

In the initial investigation into Diana's assassination, investigator John Morgan found 84 blatant lies in the Paget Report and listed them in his 2007 book, *Cover-up of a Royal Murder.*

In addition to that criminality, Morgan also published dozens of documents that were hidden from the inquest jury in a second book in 2010 entitled, *Documents the Jury Never Saw.* John Morgan was a citizen of New Zealand who was harassed relentlessly for his research until his death on November 19th, 2015

In the initial investigation into the assassination of President Kennedy, my friend, and Attorney, Mark Lane, found 108 blatant lies in the Warren Commission Report and listed them in his 1966 Bestselling book entitled *Rush to Judgement.*

No publisher in the United States would publish his fact filled book initially so he was forced to publish it in Europe. In the years that followed Lane would be harassed in the media and tormented in the JFK community by rumors that he was an informant or and operative of the CIA which was totally false. Mark Lane died on May 10th, 2016.

Both John Morgan and Mark Lane researched the truth, exposed government sponsored coverups and revealed the lies that were perpetrated on the public. As a reward for their tremendous effort in digging and telling the truth, both men were relentlessly harassed and discredited for their efforts.

Further breaking down the coincidences between the Paget Report and the Warren Commission Report are how both investigations handled the probe regarding the leading persons of interest. Within hours they pivoted away from any real investigation and blamed Henri Paul and Lee Harvey Oswald. Why?

Again, dead men tell no tales, they can't hire defense attorneys and they can't sue for false arrest. Paul and Oswald were the perfect patsies and fall guys to blame for these murders; but in the decades that followed, strong evidence has emerged, that neither of them had murdered anyone.

Besides, why actually investigate anything when it's much easier to collect your government funded paycheck and blame two dead guys who will never complain? But being killed and posthumously labeled as murderers wasn't where the similarities of Paul and Oswald ended.

Both were on the payroll as governmental intelligence informers and neither were correctly aligned in the history books or in the decades of public conciseness that followed. If they had made any of this information official, they wouldn't have been able to make their theories of a "lone nut" work.

170

In reality, Lee Harvey Oswald had been working as an operative and informant for the United States Government for years prior to JFK's murder and they knew his whereabouts and his skillset long before the assassination. This letter from the United States government clearly indicates that Lee Harvey Oswald was not a "lone gunman" and was indeed working as an operative for the American government when he was setup to take the murder wrap for the assassination of President Kennedy.

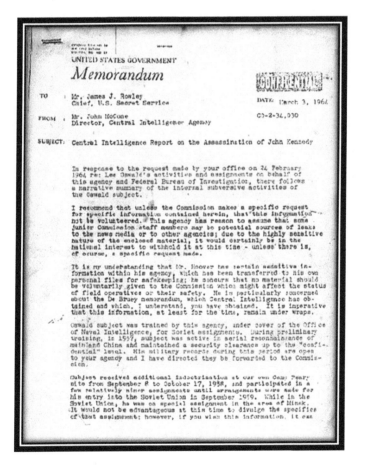

As I furthered my probe into Oswald using a highly placed source in Texas, I uncovered his Department of Defense card. Another key fact that was conveniently "missing" from the fabled Warren Commission Report. Lee Harvey Oswald was not a malcontent, an idiot or lone nut. He was working at a very high level for the CIA when they hung him out to dry.

Courtesy of the Dallas Municipal Archives and Records Center, City of Dallas,Texas

In the assassination of Princess Diana, Henri Paul has been identified by former MI6 agent Richard Tomlinson as an informant who was handsomely paid for information by many governmental intelligence agencies. His job was to feed these agencies with information on their international hotel guests.

The governments of Saudi Arabia, the United States, Israel, England and France all had paid Henri Paul for decades prior to his pre-planned murder. Tomlinson's quotes regarding Paul's role are as follows. *"It is very common for national security services to try and recruit members of security staff in the big hotels as they are very well placed to pick up information."* He continues saying that Paul was *"... a longstanding agent for MI6, an agent in terms of supplying information to MI6 about the goings on in the Ritz Hotel in return for cash and he'd been working for MI6, since, um, well I'd seen his file for the first time in 1992 and from memory he'd been working for MI6 a few years prior to that"*

The documentary Unlawful Killing elaborated on Richard Tomlinson's information with the following quote *"The inquest heard undisputed evidence of Henri Paul's connection to the French Secret Services and to Britain's MI6. So why did the coroner tell the jury in his summing up that Henri Paul had no links to the security services? Henri Paul's bank accounts show he received a total of 350,000 French Francs of unexplained income during the final months of his life, mostly from checks."*

"Why didn't the inquest establish who had written those checks or examine the transactions made on Henri Paul's five credit cards or allow the jury to see his mobile phone records? If the inquest has failed to answer one or two of these simple questions you might put it down to incompetence, but its failure even to ask many of them because the authorities already knew the answers and wanted to keep them hidden"

This evidence clearly illustrates that the Paget Report was lying when it published the following three statements.

Page 383: *"It is not known where the (FF12,565 or £1,256) cash found in (Henri's) possession on Saturday August 30 1997 came from."*

Page 820: *All of the evidence available shows that Henri Paul was not an informant for MI6 or working for them in any way."*

Page 828: *"All the evidence available showed that Henri Paul did not work for and has never had a file at MI6."*

There was no attempt or investigation by any country involved to explain why 54,900 Francs had mysteriously been deposited in Henri Paul's bank account the day of the crash or to investigate the large sum of money in his pocket when his body was recovered.

Why had the French and/or British report failed to uncover the source of the money that Henri Paul received, to interrogate the many and mysterious deposits to his bank account by check, which were easily traceable, or investigate links between the intelligence agencies and the hotel security staff?

The missing evidence seems to boggle the mind of anyone trying to get to the bottom of the possible murder of the mother of the future king of England. The answers to the above questions are simple. Don't look for what you don't want to find, especially when the facts lead right back to who hired the assassins.

The true investigation into Henri Paul, much like the true investigation into the Lee Harvey Oswald included "uncomfortable facts" that didn't fit the narrative of their one-sided investigation. These facts needed to be immediately squelched from history so they could be forever maligned as crazy, drunk, or socially despicable people by a bought off media who cooperated in on the coverup.

Conveniently, both Paul and Oswald were installed as fall guys, scapegoats and patsies while the real killers are still out there, laughing up their sleeves at the people who believe these "investigations" that were little more than expensive fairytales whose contents were peppered with confirmation bias and approved by the same people who hired their murders.

The evidence in both cases is clear. Neither Henri Paul or Lee Harvey Oswald were crazy, drunk, social misfits or despicable people; they were both working for, or working in coordination with, governmental agencies, and both were hung out to dry. The only difference between these two people is that Oswald was murdered by a bullet, and Paul was murdered in a car accident.

Another eerie parallel between these two horrendously successful setups was the governmental control of the media coverage. Walter Cronkite of CBS News was already telling the grief stricken American public that Oswald was the killer and that he acted alone before the Dallas Police could have completed their investigation into the facts.

Oswald was found to be guilty in the court of public opinion before he even spoke to an attorney. His setup was so rushed that it bypassed the entire due process of law, but if you pick up any book on the subject, he is listed as the assassin. Not a bad setup for a guy who never had a trial. Appallingly Walter Cronkite was to be remembered as "the most trusted man in America."

Henri Paul's autopsy and toxicology reports were not even finished and operatives within the French government were already feeding the world media with the erroneous tale that he killed Diana because he was driving out of control and he was "Drunk as a Pig."

The final parallel in the Paget and Warren Commission Report was that neither was accepted by the public and decades after their death's; real, unbiased, and clear-eyed investigators are still trying to find the truth as they are uncovering new evidence. These are truths that have yet to be told to the world and, if left to the international community and the global elite, never will be.

Earlier in the book I explained the details of the Bilderberg Group and what they were, but I didn't fully explain who they were controlled by and what their real purpose was. You can't have a competent conversation about the members of the Bilderbergers without first breaking down and explaining their big brother, the Federal Reserve.

Once the story of the Federal Reserve has been fully explained, the final link between the Paget Repot and the Warren Commission Report can be understood. Some view the Federal Reserve as a shadowy group of international financiers designed to serve their own interests at the expense of the middle class. Others view them as a necessary evil in the light of an ever-growing world economy. Regardless of your view, their beginnings cannot be disputed.

They were a construct of the Rothschild, Vanderbilt, and Morgan families. The Morgan family made its international fortune in England as an ally of the Rothschilds and other European financiers and one of their agents drafted the script for the Federal Reserve.

From that description, it should shock no one that the Federal Reserve Bank of New York is principally owned by five merchant banks in London chartered by the Bank of England making America nothing more than a political satellite with someone else pulling the strings of their international policy.

Irrespective of the intention or their structure they would go on to be bathed in the blood of arms dealing, murder and the rigging of American political leadership. The Federal Reserve had its beginnings all the way back in 1910 in a remote island off the coast of Georgia named Jekyll Island.

This tiny island was purchased by JP Morgan and was originally intended to be a winter getaway for the rich and famous who need a break from the rigors of the banking capital of the new world, New York City. Back then they called themselves the Jekyll Island Club, and it wasn't long before the tiny ocean getaway morphed into a secret conclave for the world's most powerful bankers.

As they sipped their drinks and twisted their oversized mustaches, they devised a new way to do what they did best - screw people out of their cash and gain total control doing it. In order to do this, these unelected robber barons had to convince someone in the United States government that America was a financially unstable country in comparison to the older and more established countries of Europe and that they could prevent the seasonal cash crunches, panics and bank failures that they had experienced.

That was the public sales pitch, but privately they lusted to get their hooks into the young country's finances. After long debates they decided to cast aside the Constitution of the United States which clearly states that *"The Congress Shall coin the money and the currency and regulate the value thereof."* and enact their plan.

178

On November 22, 1910 six of the world's most powerful men gathered. They were Senator Aldrich (Chairman of the Banking Committee), A.P. Andrews (Assistant Secretary of the United States Treasury Department), Paul Warburg (a naturalized German representing Kuhn, Loeb & Co.), Frank A. Vanderlip (president of the National City Bank of New York), Henry P. Davison (senior partner of J. P. Morgan Company), Charles D. Norton (president of the Morgan-dominated First National Bank of New York), and Benjamin Strong (representing J. P. Morgan).

This motley assortment of characters, who represented approximately one quarter of the world's wealth, would propose their takeover of the financial system named The Aldrich Bill, with the bill being sponsored by Senator Aldrich. The bill died a violent death from Democrat opposition leaders forcing the power brokers to switch to plan "B", Plan "B" meaning simply, get the Republicans to propose the same bill.

As the calendar rolled into 1912 and they continued to argue over the bill in Congress, the bankers behind it knew that they had a bigger problem. They knew that Republican President William Howard Taft would never sign the bill into law and Woodrow Wilson, who hated the Constitution, had no charisma, and couldn't beat Taft in their upcoming election. To fix this problem JP Morgan coaxed Theodore Roosevelt out of retirement to divide the Republican vote and force the Presidential Election of Woodrow Wilson.

JP Morgan and Theodore Roosevelt were more than well acquainted as Morgan's right-hand man, George Perkins, was vice-president of his bank in New York and lived at the White House during Roosevelt's term in office.

It took quite a bit of twisting and dirty dealing, but the hyper wealthy won the day and in a very short time they would not only prove to be totally ineffective but would punish America in the decades that followed.

In fact, the newly formed Federal Reserve was responsible for three of the biggest upheavals and monetary tragedies of the 20th century; World War I, the Great Depression, and World War II, and they made huge fortunes from the manipulation of all three.

Shortly after its inception came the World War I manipulation, although it had its humble beginnings long before the conflict was ever thought of. History shows us that war is the most profitable thing that an international financier can be involved in and over the last 275 years they have backed both sides of the bloodiest conflicts of the North American and European theater.

This was easy to accomplish as they had absolute power over the finances of world governments, their political parties, and their armies. Because of this, they tried to manipulate and instigate war in Europe since 1884. Many people believe that the assassination of Archduke Franz Ferdinand, who was ironically also murdered in his motorcade, was the work of international bankers to begin the conflict.

After the war in Europe had been raging for many years and the financiers hàd bankrupted their central banks, they realized that the only treasure that remained was the economic frontier of the United States, so the newly formed Federal Reserve, which is no more federal than Federal Express, began to flex its muscle.

Although Woodrow Wilson initially pledged that America was going to remain neutral, he was easily swayed into the fight by his confidante, best friend and "alter ego", Edward Mandell House. Colonel House, as he was called, was a communist plant in the Wilson Administration.

He, like the Federal Reserve, was another unelected brain trust who had targeted Wilson for friendship earlier in his career. His intention was to domineer the American President away from our current form of government and toward the Parliamentary system, where the Executive and the Legislative Branches of government were the same.

This was covered at length in volume III of my book series, *Who Murdered FDR?*. By manipulating America into World War I, the big bankers were able to drag the war out and sell guns to one side while making loans to the other. In reality, war has nothing to do with bullets or generals, it's all about the dollars and how they can be manipulated.

This was illustrated by the hearings of Senator Gerald Nye where he cross examined the biggest bankers, arms brokers and industrialists revealing their profits. World War I was nothing more than a profit-making venture designed to build their wealth and pad the coffers of their banking institutions.

The same formula was used by Jacob Schiff, Max Warburg and JP Morgan during the Russian Revolution as they financed both Trotsky and Lenin with billions of dollars. They'll let nothing stand in the way of prolonging the conflict to keep the money rolling in.

A little over a decade after the passage of the Federal Reserve, America saw the biggest depression in its history and it wasn't prevented by "The Fed", it was planned by them. For the 18 months prior to the crash of 1929 the Federal Reserve increased the supply of money by 62% causing people to buy and sell - pledge and borrow - as if the good times would never end. Then the bankers pulled the plug on the money supply and the common people lost everything; stocks, bonds, homes, cars, savings – everything.

This created the perfect scenario for "those in the know" to buy securities at rock bottom prices positioning themselves for the flood of inevitable profits when the economic tragedy ended. These events aren't the paranoid ravings of conspiracy theorists, these are historical facts that happened.

The following two quotes speak volumes. American Economist and Nobel Prize recipient Milton Friedman said that the Federal Reserve caused the Great Depression by reducing the amount of money in circulation. *"Depositors all over the country were frightened about the safety of their funds and rushed to withdraw them. There were runs. There were failures of banks by the droves and all the time the Federal Reserve System stood idly by when it had the power, and the duty, and the responsibility to provide the cash that would have enabled the banks to meet the insistent demands of their depositors without closing their doors."*

US Congressman and Chairman of The House Banking Committee, Louis McFadden agreed saying *"The Great Depression was a carefully contrived occurrence by international bankers seeking to bring about a condition of despair so that they might emerge as the rulers of us all"*

During that time banking insider, and JFK's father, Joseph Kennedy, saw his wealth balloon from $3.5 million in 1929 to over $110 million in the four years that followed. It's the greatest of ironies that the same power brokers who made the Kennedy family wealthy beyond imagination would also arrange for the murder of President John F. Kennedy, one of their sons.

JFK was caught in the crossfire of the Federal Reserve as he was trying to rein in their power with the issuance of Executive Order 11110. Kennedy signed the bill into law on June 4, 1963 which transferred power from the Federal Reserve to the United States Department of the Treasury which replaced Federal Reserve Notes with Silver Certificates.

There was more to JFK's assassination than this singular event which I will cover in depth in my next book entitled, *Who Murdered JFK?*, but this was one of the major catalysts. Tragic as it was, JFK's orchestrated murder wasn't their first. In fact, he was the third US President to be targeted.

President Andrew Jackson was an outspoken opponent of the Federal Reserve and the first assassination target of the bankers. On January 30th, 1835 an assassin connected to international bankers named Richard Lawrence stuck two pistols in Jackson's belly and pulled the triggers simultaneously.

Both pistols misfired, and Jackson would go on to kill the country's central bank. It was a feat that he deemed his greatest accomplishment and one that he was so proud of that he had the words "I killed the Bank" engraved on his gravestone.

Abraham Lincoln was the second Presidential assassination target of international bankers as he struggled financially to preserve the Union, without the finances to accomplish it.

In desperation, honest Abe went to the big bankers on Wall Street who agreed to produce the funds but at a whopping 36 percent interest. Lincoln took a less expensive rout choosing to have Congress issue the money instead.

These "greenbacks" were only backed by a congressional promise and didn't involve paying the international banker's interest. Despite what the history books claim, when John Wilkes Booth shot Lincoln it was largely because the bankers wanted control of the nation's money.

In fact, historians now believe that Lincoln's vice president, and successor, Andrew Johnson, planned the assassination with John Wilkes Booth as he had struck a deal with the Wall Street bankers so that they could profit from the reconstruction of the nation and the great migration west.

A financially independent America posed a serious threat to the financial powers of the world and no one said it better during the American Civil War than Germany's Chancellor Otto von Bismarck *"the division of the United States was decided by the high financial powers of Europe they were afraid that the US would upset their financial domination over the world they saw tremendous booty if they could substitute too feeble democracies burdened with debt to the financiers in place of the vigorous Republic sufficient unto herself"*

This is the back story and a brief history lesson of the Federal Reserve and their hand selected fraternity called the Bilderberg Group. A group that has so much power that it escapes the media's attention everywhere in the world that they decide to meet to divvy up their share of the profits.

Imagine 150 Boy Scout leaders gathering in your town and giving advanced notice that they will be there. Wouldn't every media outlet be there asking a few questions? Naturally they'd at least be a little curious, but curiosity, in this case seems to end. Why? Aren't you at least a little curious what these globally assembled power brokers are doing in your town?

The secrecy and backstage passes never end for these privileged few who are the hidden cabal that are actually running the world, irrespective of who you think your elected leader is. This is where the final juncture between the murder of Princess Diana and the Paget Report and the murder of JFK and the Warren Commission Report collide.

Both of these people stood in the way of the international bankers and their cash cows. Princess Diana was becoming more and more political on an international scale and was reducing the need for arms. There would be no way for the international tycoons to make huge profits from funding both sides of the conflict in Bosnia, Angola or in many other places that she visited, as they had done hundreds of times in the past.

Diana was creating peace, not war, and there are no profits to be made from peace. Also, whoever controls Diana – controls the world, and the bank of London, who controls almost all of the Federal Reserve financiers, wanted no part of their arch enemy, Muhammad Al-Fayed. Diana needed to be murdered in a car ride through a tunnel which served their needs perfectly.

JFK stepped on so many toes throughout his short Presidency that it's almost impossible to list them all, but possibly his most dangerous action was against the Federal Reserve and their immensely profitable monopoly on the creation of America's paper money.

By signing Executive Order 11110 he thumbed his nose at the world's most wealthy, most powerful and most dangerous men. That order killed the golden goose for the Federal Reserve bankers by replacing their Federal Reserve Notes with Silver Certificates that were going to be issued by the Treasury Department with no interest owed.

Both Diana and JFK stood in the way of the world's most power men making their wealth and both paid the price with their mortal souls. Enviably, the word came down from the bankers, to their minions in their respective governments who hired their assassination teams so they could get them out of their way.

Perhaps Meyer Rothschild of the Rothschild banking family said it best, *"give me control of a nation's monetary system and I care not who writes their laws."* By now it should seem obvious that there is no political party or system of government that rules the world.

There are no Democrats or Republicans, there is no Conservative Party or Labour Party – there are only haves and have nots, and unless you're seated at their table, you're on the outside looking in. Both the Paget Report and the Warren Commission Report were reinvestigated, and the determination was the exact opposite of the original version.

The London's Royal Courts of Justice who reinvestigated the French Dossier concluded that Princess Diana was killed due to an "unlawful killing" - the court equivalent of manslaughter.

The Select Committee on Assassination of the United States House of Representatives reinvestigated the Warren Commission Report and established that there was a second shooter in the JFK assassination.

A second shooter who, acting in concert with the first shooter, fulfilled the legal definition of conspiracy. Stop the debate – the United States government admitted that JFK was murdered in a conspiracy. However, in both cases, no effort was made by either government to find, solve, investigate, or further elaborate on the murderers.

Odd, since the United States Constitution and the Magna Carta mirror each other in numerous ways including criminal investigation procedures and the criminal process. Both countries abandoned any investigation into the murders violating their own civil, criminal, and governmental laws.

That is strikingly similar to the odd behavior of the coroners, police, crime scene investigators, gunshot experts, automobile crash experts and toxicologists who also conveniently, and suddenly, forgot how to do their jobs. Why? Because any solid investigation into these murders would lead directly back to global elite who gave the order in the first place and anyone probing that far would surely be fired, smeared or murdered themselves.

You won't find the smoking gun because they don't want you to know that the same people who were in charge of launching the investigations and show trials were the murderers themselves. Any government who could chose, without legality, which case to investigate and which case to ignore is flowing a separate set of rules than we are.

In other words, we are not their citizens, we are their property, they own us, and we'd better learn to mind our place, and that's the real message that is being sent. Is there any wonder that the Internal Revenue Service uses the term "inventory" to describe the tax paying citizens of the United States? That's how they view us; as nameless, faceless numbers for them to contort and manage to their liking.

So, the faster we let the power brokers return to the normalcy of fixing elections, financial sodomy, slaughter and military conflict the easier it will be on all of us. So, the next time an event like this happens, just realize who's behind it, shrug your shoulders, and move on - because we're powerless to stop them.

Human beings are an interesting breed. We admire things of beauty and righteousness so much that we can't help but destroy them. When we see a butterfly fluttering through our garden, we have to catch it and touch its wings and then it never flies again. We do the same thing with the brightest lightning bugs that dance before us in the blackest of warm summer nights. The first thing we do is put them in a jar. A jar that will eventually become their coffin.

The same goes for the intentional destruction of churches, cathedrals, synagogues, mosques, and mandirs around the world because certain people pray to a different invisible man then we do. The same can be said for the planned and coordinated defacing and destruction of monuments and statues, which are tremendous works of art, that were made at the expense of millions of dollars and thousands of hours of painstaking labor.

Do we find a different place to put them? No, we smash them to the ground and spit on them as we continue to behave as secretly funded savages, fools, and ignorant spoiled brats. Does anyone profit when the creation of art is destroyed? I think not.

Somehow in our best intentions we have managed to murder Jesus, MLK, Elvis, JFK, Princess Diana, FDR, and countless others who have made us laugh, smile and brought hope to millions of people. These are the oddest examples of behavior for a species who claims that they desire peace, love, tolerance, and justice when we are doing the exact opposite.

Princess Diana's compassion for the sick, underprivileged, and injured, combined with her tireless drive for world peace bought her a one-way ticket out of the looney bin that we call the human race. Beyond any doubt, she was clearly too good to exist in this world.